WANTED: EXTREME CHRISTIANS

Powerful Lessons for Those Who Dare to Obey Christ Completely

STEPHEN HILL

ARDENT

P R E S S

Published by Ardent Press, Inc.
Dallas, Texas, U.S.A.
Printed in the U.S.A.

Cover and Inside Design by Robert Williams
Edited by Nancy Justice, Rose Decaen and Christi Goeser

Library of Congress Cataloging-in-Publication Data
Hill, Stephen, 1954-
  Wanted, Extreme Christians / Stephen Hill.
    p. cm.
  ISBN 0-8307-2911-9 (trade paper)
  1. Christian life—Assemblies of God authors. 2. Hill,
Stephen, 1954-   I. Title.
  BV4501.3 .H55 2002
  243—dc21   2001008154

1 2 3 4 5 6 7 8 9 10 11 12 13 14 15 / 09 08 07 06 05 04 03 02

Rights for publishing this book in other languages are contracted by Ardent Press, Inc.

DEDICATION

All of us are responsible for living our lives in a manner that glorifies Christ and brings honor to His kingdom. As a Christian, I sense a deep responsibility to live each moment in a way that pleases my Lord. He has placed me on this planet at this time in history for a purpose.

All Christians will be held accountable for what they have done with their time, talent and treasure. We may come from different lands, different times and different cultures, but there are three things we can all be certain of: (1) one day we will all be together; (2) time, as we know it, will be no more; and (3) all our works will be judged by fire.

The stark reality of this truth is what motivated the late evangelist and my dear friend Leonard Ravenhill to say, "On that day you had better hope you're not standing knee-deep in ashes."

After the Judgment will come an event I've longed for all my Christian life: Every believer from every age, tongue, and tribe will be gathered together and seated at the Marriage Supper of the Lamb. It will be dinner with Deity. Perhaps I'll have the privilege of sitting across the banquet table from a martyr, one who faithfully served Jesus and boldly glorified God—not only in the way he or she lived but also in the way he or she died. This martyr could be from Bible days or modern times. Regardless, this person will have loved Christ more than his or her life and died to the world—literally.

I guess you could say I'm in the prime of life, age-wise. Should the Lord tarry, I hope to live many more years and expect to do much more for God. While I continue fulfilling God's call on my life, I'm certain others are fulfilling theirs. Some of them are even shedding their blood for the cause of Christ. It is to them, the Christian martyrs of today and yesterday, that I dedicate this book. These unwavering soldiers of the Cross have paved the way to heaven with their blood. They truly exemplify and have lived out extreme Christianity – they dared to follow Christ completely.

Table of Contents

WANTED: EXTREME CHRISTIANS

INTRODUCTION

"Jeri and I have been married 21 years, and we've moved 21 times." A sea of bewildered, shocked faces stared back at us. I was the keynote speaker at a pastors' and lay leaders' luncheon in Seattle, Washington, two years ago. Theirs was a typical reaction to that statement which I often share with the groups I speak to. I went on to explain: "My wife and I have been missionary evangelists for over 20 years. As church planters we go to cities and villages in South America, Europe and Russia to start churches and then turn them over to national pastors before moving on."

"We know what it's like to face the unknown, start from scratch, establish friendships, wrestle with demons, preach the Cross and salvation only through Jesus, have the critics blast us, see people run to the Lord for forgiveness, ground new believers in the Word, watch a small body of believers grow into a thriving congregation and then leave, only to start the process all over again."

On this particular day, I was sharing about the cost of revival. I then made the statement, "If you want revival, it will cost you everything!" Their collective gasp was seasoned with only a few "Amens." I knew I had struck a chord in the hearts of these precious believers.

What they were hearing from me could be defined as "extreme." It's a word that's become an integral part of today's intense, thrill-seeking society. We hear of extreme adventures, extreme sports, and extreme roller coasters. By definition, "extreme" means "very intense; far beyond the norm; radical."

In actuality, our audience was hearing about the "extreme" lifestyle of two soldiers radically sold out to Jesus. All Jeri and I do is follow the mandates of our Commander in Chief, which is normal behavior for any committed soldier. Our calling then, and today, is very personal and passionate.

Each and every Christian must listen to and obey the Lord. What God calls us to do might be extreme to some but simplistic and easy to others. I have friends who've been called to difficult, dangerous areas of the world—I'm talking about dungeons of darkness, places where the blood of martyrs runs deep. But my friends count it an honor to give their lives for the One who bled and died for them.

Others work in primitive jungles, paddling through snake-infested waters searching for remote tribes lost from society. With a Bible in one hand and a brush-slashing machete in the other, they forge their way quoting Acts 1:8, "But you shall receive power when the Holy Spirit has come upon you; and you shall be My witnesses both in Jerusalem, and in all Judea and Samaria, and even to the remotest part of the earth."

Of course, in the dense, dark forest, nobody but God hears these missionaries. I ask you, is this extreme or normal?

How totally ironic that today's thrill seekers and adventure junkies can log onto extreme vacation websites and sign up for their dream trip to no-man's land. They load up their brand-new, state-of-the-art gear, hop a plane to some remote location, take a safari jeep miles into the jungle, board a dugout canoe and make their way down some uncharted river. They set up camp, and the next morning take off hiking, only to run into dedicated missionaries who've been working with the local tribes for 15 years in hand-me-down clothing and worn-out shoes. Let's talk extreme.

Was it extreme for David Wilkerson, back in 1958, to storm, with Bible in hand, into a New York City courtroom during the trial of a handful of hell-bound gang members, and plead to the judge, "Respect me as a minister of the Gospel, and let me have one moment, please"? Wilkerson was forcibly led from the courtroom, but reporters recorded his intentions. All he wanted was to talk with gang members about their salvation. Does that sound intense and fanatical to you? Or does it fit with your idea of Biblical obedience?

If you haven't heard the fascinating story of Reverend Wilkerson, founder of Teen Challenge, read his book *The Cross and the Switchblade*. Be careful though—it's far beyond the "norm." Sadly though, for many in today's church body, what should be normal is often labeled as extreme.

You're about to read the story of an extreme journey. I begin this book on my twenty-fifth spiritual birthday. On October 28, 1975, a dear Lutheran minister led me to the Cross of Jesus Christ, and my life was changed forever. Little did I know then what was ahead for me. Jesus has taken me places I never dreamed of. Now, reader, I want to take you with me to visit the mountains and the valleys. I want you to experience the sights and sounds of our crusades around the world. I want you to savor the thrill of victory as you read about thousands being saved and sense the power in Jesus' name as demons flee in fear. Accompany me as I journey from my drug addiction to my Jesus addiction; from my basic training in Teen Challenge to receiving my marching orders at David Wilkerson's Twin Oaks Academy. Watch Jeri and me go from comfortable church pews to calloused city streets, to the white-hot, devil chasin' revival in Argentina and then to the fiery soul-savin' outpouring in Pensacola, Florida.

It's impossible for me to write about everything that's happened to us over the last 25 years of ministry. I'd love to tell you about when we opened our home to the homeless one Thanksgiving; when Jeri fell into a manhole while walking down a street in Costa Rica; and when we experienced heartbreak over our miscarriages on the mission field.

As I have sifted through our past to write this book, I've laughed and cried. And I've prayed and asked God to help write what would be most beneficial to you, the reader.

Each chapter contains firsthand accounts of how we experienced scriptural truths up close and personal. Sprinkled throughout are powerful truths I call Extreme Personal Lessons that we've gleaned from years of ministry.

Don't worry—I won't get bogged down in deep theology or try to impress you by waxing eloquent. This book is intended to be read and enjoyed. Hopefully, you'll also be challenged and motivated in your spiritual walk.

I've purposely avoided quoting other authors and flooding each page with footnotes. I just want to share some powerful lessons for those who dare to obey Christ completely.

But before you turn another page, let me share a personal conviction. My friend, I don't see myself as one who has done anything "great" for Jesus. I blush to be mentioned in the same sentence as some of the world-shaking evangelists of yesteryear and sincerely cannot stomach being included in someone's lofty list of great men and women of God, especially after having studied their humble and sacrificial lives.

I cannot change the fact that most Christians are not on fire for Jesus, but I can stir the embers and throw some fresh logs on the fire. That's what I want to do through this book—ignite a fire in your heart. Maybe, just maybe, you will grab a word or two of inspiration from these pages and launch into the deep for Jesus. Perhaps my 25 adventurous years with Jesus will make your next 25 years more adventurous.

May terms like "radical," "intense" and "beyond the norm" someday identify your life. These are the days for extreme Christianity.

Sin Is A Tattletale

CHAPTER ONE

EXTREME LESSON:

Sooner or later, the divine penalty for sinful behavior must be paid.

"For the wages of sin is death, but the free gift of God is eternal life in Christ Jesus our Lord."

ROMANS 6:23

He stood in the midst of the crowd, piercing the air with his screams and sending shock waves through those sitting close by. "Help me!" he cried. "Somebody please help me!"

I was preaching to several thousand people at a Friday night service in Copenhagen, Denmark, when this young man in his mid-20s decided to interrupt me.

It was a normal occurrence in our crusade meetings. After all, this wasn't a sleepy Sunday morning service in suburban America. This was a Holy Ghost revival meeting and people had come from near and far seeking a touch from God. Some would wait patiently until the prayer time at the end of the service, while others, like this young man, could not.

For many that day, the man's plea for immediate attention was extremely uncomfortable. After all, who would have the nerve to interrupt the preaching of God's Word? Who would dare make such a spectacle of themselves?

An usher raced to the young man's side, put his arm around his shoulder and whispered to him, "It's gonna be alright. Sit down with me. In just a few minutes, the evangelist will pray with you."

The usher patiently sat by his side, concerned that he might turn violent, but hopeful that his life would change. He needed to hear the message.

We've all seen this kind of guy—hair matted from sleeping outside on the ground, rumpled clothes smelling of alcohol, threadbare shoes. His eyes were sunken, and he hadn't shaved in weeks. But it didn't really matter—who cared? This man represented the dregs of society, and he was just one of the millions of people around the world who have dropped out and many wish they would just drop dead as well.

They hang out under bridges and in alleyways. They panhandle in the streets and hold "Will Work for Food" signs at busy intersections. They display their goods in the seedier side of town, hoping to turn enough tricks to support their habits. They're the castaways everyone wants to cast even further away.

Society calls them *wasted*, but our Savior calls them *wanted*. Jesus didn't specify a certain culture, ethnic group or social status when He said, "And I, if I be lifted up from the earth, will draw all men to Myself" (John 12:32). He meant *all*, as in everyone.

Remember this about the prodigals among us: Somewhere there's a worried dad waiting for his wayward son to come home. That hardened, painted-up street hooker is some distraught mother's lost daughter; to the police she's a menace, but to Mama back home she's her little girl.

That young man had somehow made it to our crusade. When he stood up and screamed, everyone just stared—some even glared. Whenever this happens in our services, I am reminded of Bartimaeus, the blind beggar of Jericho who was healed by Jesus.

We meet Bartimaeus in Mark 10:46, sitting by the highway begging (sound familiar?). He was in desperate need of a touch from God—and knew it!—and was determined to get Jesus' attention. Mark writes, "When [Bartimaeus] heard that it was Jesus the Nazarene, he began to cry out and say, 'Jesus, Son of David, have mercy on me!'" (v. 47). His cries filled the air but were seemingly ineffective—the Lord kept walking on by. The crowd rebuked Bartimaeus and told him to shut up (also sound familiar?). They were certain of the Lord's decision to pass him by.

But, according to Mark 10:48, Bartimaeus yelled even louder. The result? Jesus stopped (v. 49). This blind man's sincere, relentless cries actually stopped the Lord in His tracks.

Jesus turned and replied, "What do you want Me to do for you?" Bartimaeus immediately responded, "Rabboni, I want to regain my sight!" (v. 51).

Jesus granted his request, and I know why. This belligerent blind man had demonstrated his belief in God by going after Him, even in the midst of serious persecution. He wasn't about to give in to the pessimistic opinions of others. After all, he was blind, not they. He was going to get a touch from God, and nothing was going to stop him. This brings us to our first Extreme Personal Lesson.

EXTREME PERSONAL LESSON:

When you want something from God, go after Him. Oftentimes God is testing our faith to see how determined we are. Your willingness to knock and keep on knocking will eventually result in Jesus opening the door.

The same was true of our young man in the crusade. Many in the crowd wanted him to shut up and "act normal." Some were probably thinking, *Surely the preacher will have this derelict removed from our revival service.* If the guy had turned violent or produced a weapon, then, of course, we would have dealt with him differently. But here was someone disturbing us because he was desperate, not defiant.

Feeling the Lord's compassion, I simply said, "Have a seat, my friend. Jesus is in this place and He's here to meet your need. Nobody cares for you like Jesus." He sat down and got calm, but several minutes later was right back up screaming, "Help me!"

"In just a minute," I answered back. The usher once again sat him down. God's Word was being preached, and this lost soul needed to hear it. I've learned over the years the riveting truth of Hebrews 4:12: "For the word of God is living and active and sharper than any two-edged sword, and piercing as far as the division of soul and spirit, of both joints and marrow, and able to judge the thoughts and intentions of the heart."

This man needed to hear the Word of God. His soul needed to be pierced with the message of the Cross, Jesus' shed blood and God's love. Romans 10:13-14 explains it this way: "For 'Whoever will call upon the name of the LORD will be saved.' How then shall they call upon Him in whom they have not believed? And how shall they believe in Him whom they have not heard? And how shall they hear without a preacher?"

After the sermon was finished and the altar call given, I saw a scene I've witnessed in cities and towns around the world. Hundreds of people immediately rushed forward. Many were actually running; others were diving to the carpet.

Our vocal visitor was the first one to arrive, tears streaming down his face. He had heard how Jesus shed His blood for him. He had heard that sin separated him from God and that only through the blood of Jesus could he receive forgiveness. He had listened to me explain how sin destroys, how God demands repentance and how repentance means to turn from our wicked ways and change our lives. The altars were then opened. He felt the presence of God—he was ready.

EXTREME PERSONAL LESSON:

Sin separates you from God. Sin is anything Jesus wouldn't do. When you have sinned, learn to repent immediately and determine in your heart not to do it again.

Our young friend prayed. Jesus forgave. Several serious saints of God gathered around, covering him in prayer. He stayed until just about everyone had left. He had nowhere to go. A bridge down the road was home, and scraps of food from passersby kept him alive. He had a choice—go back to that or stay with this. The sweet presence of God in this auditorium was far better than the world outside.

I then saw in his back pocket a crumpled copy of my testimony booklet *Stone Cold Heart*. He said someone had given it to him and invited him to the crusade. He had read how Jesus changed my life and wanted to experience the same type of deliverance. He wasn't disappointed.

A church member then offered him a place to stay. I explained to this excited young man that it wouldn't be easy to live the Christian life. Now, I wasn't trying to discourage him—I was just being honest. "Coming to a crusade is one thing," I said. "Getting the sin out and staying clean is another. If you're serious, you'll be back tomorrow night." He was—and the following nights, too. Within a few days he was well on his way to the most exciting adventure known to man: the Christian life.

Isolated incident? Hardly. I've seen similar scenarios played out all over the world. People come to a revival meeting with a desperate desire for change. They're suffering from the serious side effects of sin. Oftentimes their lives are spinning out of control, and they are teetering on the brink of death.

They've learned the hard way some rough lessons about sin and three undeniable truths about giving in to the lusts of the flesh: (1) sin takes you farther than you ever intended to go; (2) sin keeps you longer than you ever intended to stay; (3) sin costs you more than you ever intended to spend.

At some point in our crusades, people usually hear me issue this challenge: "If you get serious with God, He'll get serious with you. The ball is in your court. Jesus died for *you*, now what are *you* going to do for Him? He came down from heaven 2,000 years ago for you, and now it's time for you to come to Him!" The altars then fill with lost and dying souls seeking a touch from the living God.

We experience the same results in every evangelistic outreach of our ministry. Our television program draws sinners from all over the world to repentance. Our books have melted some pretty hard hearts. Just a few days ago, we received a letter from a prison inmate. He had found a copy of my testimony in the trash, pulled it out and read it. The thought occurred to him, *If God can do that for Steve, He can do that for me.* The inmate prayed; God forgave.

Where does my passion for the lost come from? What motivates me to continue crying out for those dying out? Why do we see the rich from Wall Street and the poor from down the street in our meetings? Why can city lawyers be found right next to city losers, kneeling and weeping tears of repentance? What is it that causes a backslidden Christian, saturated with secret sin, to flee into the arms of Jesus in front of thousands of onlookers? Aren't they concerned about what others might think? What motivates a pastor, attending our service with members of his own congregation, to come forward, even though his parishioners are present?

The answer, my friend, is found in one word: "conviction." True, life-altering, God-sent, Holy Ghost conviction. People get hit by the arrows of the Lord and, like our crusade friend, are compelled to repent.

My knowledge of sin and its sobering consequences comes from years of personal, firsthand experience. I have compassion for the lost because I'm a survivor of a lifestyle that should have killed me. The booklet our friend had in his pocket told my story—and it's not an uncommon testimony.

I was your typical rebellious teen who fell big-time for the devil's manipulative ways. When I shoplifted from stores, the devil said I would never get caught. When I adorned myself with a red robe, lit the candles in our Lutheran church and later stole from the offering plates, the devil said there was plenty of money and it wouldn't be missed. When I started drinking beer, the devil said I would never become an alcoholic. When I took my first hit of marijuana, the devil said it would never lead to heavier drugs. When I began experimenting with drugs, the devil said I would never fall for hard narcotics.

John 8:44 warns us how much of a liar the devil is: "You are of your father the devil, and you want to do the desires of your father. He was a murderer from the beginning, and does not stand in the truth, because there is no truth in him. Whenever he speaks a lie, he speaks from his own nature; for he is a liar, and the father of lies."

The enemy led me like a lamb to the slaughter. My secret little sins began to tell on me. Yes, sin is a tattletale. Numbers 32:23 is as relevant today as it was in Old Testament time: "Behold, you have sinned against the LORD, and be sure your sin will find you out."

Sin waits for just the right moment to move in for the kill. Sin caresses your hand, kisses you on the cheek and whispers empty promises into your love-struck ear. It woos you into its bedchamber, lulls you to sleep and then stabs you in the back. It promises you everything and leaves you with nothing.

I came from a typical middle-class family. I was born in Ankara, Turkey. My father had served as a captain in the military. By the time I was born, however, he was a civilian, stationed in Turkey under the Department of the U.S. Army. We later moved to the States, where I grew up in Huntsville, Alabama, with two sisters and a brother. I started drinking alcohol at age 10, started using drugs at 12 and was a full-blown drug addict by 16.

Like someone starving for food, I consumed every drug I could get my hands on. I would beg, borrow and even steal to get drugs. But there was one thing I had promised myself to never do and that was to inject drugs. I was too smart for that. Many of my buddies had experienced overdoses; some had even died.

That would never happen to me.

Even so, there was no stopping my downward slide, and eventually I broke my promise. Soon I was tying off my arm, jamming a needle into the waiting vessel and pushing the poison into my bloodstream.

Remember what I said earlier? Sin will take you farther than you ever intended to go, keep you longer than you ever intended to stay and cost you more than you ever intended to spend. I had no idea how dangerously close I had been to death until I recently heard what a former neighbor, a registered nurse, had to say about that time in my life:

I've known Steve since 1960. I baby-sat for him and three siblings, and our mothers were dear friends. We were all aware of his problems, all through high school it was common knowledge that he used drugs.

One fall afternoon in 1975 Steve's mom called to see if I could help him, since I'm a nurse. Steve was propped up in bed, surrounded by boxes of morphine tubexes (the same kind used in the hospital). He had four half-empty syringes still stuck in his veins. There was an empty bottle of sleeping pills on the bed next to him. I asked his sister how many he had taken. She told me she had the prescription filled the night before and they were powerful barbiturates. He had taken all of them in less than 24 hours. His sister also said he had injected a large quantity of morphine in the same period. His pupils were pinpoint, and his skin was gray and cold. His nail beds were blue. His respirations were approximately two per minute.

I told Steve's mother he needed to be taken to the emergency room immediately, but his mother and sister were afraid he would be arrested and not taken care of properly. So I worked with him for about two hours. I stimulated him by talking to him, slapping his face, and washing him with hot and cold towels. At one point I threw a cup of cold water on him. He finally began to respond. He started to move his arms and legs and begin to talk. I've never seen anyone with such a massive overdose of drugs live to tell about it. I thank God he was able to overcome his problems and come back from the brink of death.

This dear neighbor probably saved my life that day. Of course, that was not the devil's plan. His modus operandi has not changed for thousands of years. The Bible tells us, "The thief comes only to steal, and kill, and destroy; I came that they might have life, and might have it abundantly" (John 10:10).

For me, however, the ultimate goal of the destroyer's well-executed efforts was about to be thwarted.

For years my dear mom faithfully prayed for me. I criss-crossed the country several times searching for fulfillment, craving and searching for a better high. But it seemed the more she prayed, the worse off I got. She clung to her hope and faith in Jesus and continued to intercede. Little did she know how loud and clear her cries were heard in heaven and how powerful the hand of God would be in her son's life. But before sharing my deliverance, I must insert an Extreme Personal Lesson for all those parents with a wayward child.

EXTREME PERSONAL LESSON:

You are in God's perfect will when praying for the lost. God doesn't want any to perish, but all to come to repentance. Don't give up. Remember, the prodigal son was in the pigpen – the lowest point of his life – before he came home. Keep praying for your lost loved ones.

There's a powerful promise in 1 John 5:14-15 that speaks directly to this petition. Allow these words to blow fresh wind into your intercessory sails: "And this is the confidence which we have before Him, that, if we ask anything according to His will, He hears us. And if we know that He hears us in whatever we ask, we know that we have the requests which we have asked from Him."

God was hearing Ann Hill's cries for her son on a Saturday morning in October 1975. I was 21 years old and had recently moved into my mom's house in Huntsville. My younger sister, Susie, was the only other sibling left at home; Marcia was now married and George had moved to California.

My years of drug abuse were taking their toll. My body was in spastic convulsions and I was breaking out in hot and cold sweats. The torment was unbearable and I was screaming for help. My mom rushed to my side, wiping me down with cold washcloths, attempting to relieve the agony. Nothing could be done.

Thoughts of suicide flooded my mind. I thought of friends who had died similar deaths. My chosen lifestyle of drugs, alcohol and rebellion was ending in tragedy. The curtains of my life were about to close.

This continued for several days. Although I had experienced similar symptoms in the past, this particular occasion was different. It was as if my body and mind were screaming in unison, "It's over. We quit!"

On Tuesday, October 28, Mom decided to get some help and called Hugh Mozingo, a young Lutheran minister at her church. I had met him once before but had blown him off, totally uninterested in whatever he had to say about God.

EXTREME PERSONAL LESSON:

You never know when the day of salvation will occur for a lost soul. You must be sensitive to the Holy Spirit and be ready to obey God when the call comes.

Hugh arrived at our house almost immediately. My body was still convulsing as if being jolted by electricity. Hugh didn't say much, but what he did say was exactly what I needed to hear.

"Steve, I can't help you, but I know Someone who can. His name is Jesus and He's here to deliver you. Pray with me."

Any other time I would have cussed him or dissed him, but this time I was ready: "For He says, 'At the acceptable time I listened to you, and on the day of salvation I helped you'; behold, now is 'the acceptable time,' behold, now is 'the day of salvation'" (2 Cor. 6:2).

I found myself saying aloud the name of Jesus over and over again. My body was dying, but my spirit was ready for life. I wanted to be set free. Just as Bartimaeus craved his sight, I craved deliverance. Just as Bartimaeus caught the Lord's attention, my cries demanded the gaze of God.

As I pleaded for deliverance, all heaven came down! The presence of Jesus Christ filled the room! Within a few seconds I felt brand-new! The convulsions that had racked my body for days ceased . . . *in the name of Jesus*. The emptiness I had felt for years was filled in seconds . . . *in the name of Jesus*. The confusion that had plagued me for over a decade was replaced by peace . . . *in the name of Jesus*. Hatred and bitterness gave way to love and forgiveness . . . *in the name of Jesus*.

Within a few moments I was a brand-new person, a child of God. He jerked me off that hell-bound train and placed me on the road to heaven. According to His Word, "He brought me up out of the pit of destruction, out of the miry clay; and He set my feet upon a rock, making my footsteps firm. And He put a new song in my mouth, a song of praise to our God; many will see and fear, and will trust in the LORD" (Ps. 40:2-3).

Looking back, I realize how stupid I had been to believe that my rebellious behavior would never carry serious consequences. Now when I meet young people who toy with drugs and then say it's just innocent fun, my heart bleeds for them. Despite how simple things may seem at first, the end result of sinful behavior always brings tragedy.

God's Word warns that sin will separate us from God: "Behold, the LORD's hand is not so short that it cannot save; neither is His ear so dull that it cannot hear. But your iniquities have made a separation between you and your God, and your sins have hidden His face from you, so that He does not hear" (Isa. 59:1-2).

Take it from me—separation from God is a very lonely place to be. You don't want to go there.

This is just the beginning of *Wanted: Extreme Christians*. We're just starting to learn about the wages of sin and the power of our Savior. I trust you have made a decision to repent of sin and become an on-fire follower of Jesus. If you have, then get ready—this book is for you! The following pages are full of powerful lessons for those who dare to obey Christ completely.

Go Directly to Jail

CHAPTER TWO

EXTREME LESSON:

God Allows us to pass through difficult situations in order to achieve His purpose for our lives

---

"And we know that God causes all things to work together for the good to those who love God, to those who are called according to His purpose."

ROMANS 8:28

When our friends face major trials in life, we're quick to quote them Paul's words from Romas 8:28. "Brother, you've gotta just trust the Lord," we say. "He'll get you through this. Remember, all things work together for the good to them that love God."

We're spiritual dynamos when it comes to dishing out counsel for others, but then we throw a full-blown pity party when we face trouble. As long as life is smooth sailing, we behave like great men and women of faith, but the minute a storm heads our way we throw up our hands and scream, "Jesus, why is this happening to me? I can't take it anymore! Don't You care?"

Rough times in the Christian life are inevitable. But Peter instructs us to rejoice in the midst of them: "Beloved, do not be surprised at the fiery ordeal among you, which comes upon you for your testing, as though some strange thing were happening to you; but to the degree that you share the sufferings of Christ, keep on rejoicing; so that also at the revelation of His glory, you may rejoice with exultation" (1 Pet. 4:12-13).

Each one of our trials is unique in design and designated in purpose. They keep us humble and serve to remind us that we need each other. When handled with care, our trials bring glory to Christ.

Perhaps our constant struggle to overcome difficulties is one of the reasons God has blessed the Church with "senior saints." These dear folks may be up in years, but they're gold mines of godly wisdom. Oftentimes they've been through more trials in their life than many of us ever will. They've fought the fight and run the race—they've just about finished their course. Physically they may be weak, but spiritually they have the strength of Olympic athletes.

The Lord knows how many times I've leaned on the spiritual shoulders of senior saints. I see their stories as historical road markers of life—they've been there, done that. By taking the time to listen, I've unearthed hidden treasures. A few moments of quality counsel with them seems to calm any storms brewing around me, because they breathe peace. Their sweet voices speak from a depth that we have yet to reach as they share stories of how God delivered them from the fiery furnace. Then they calmly explain how devastating some trials have been—sometimes tears silently trickle down their weathered cheeks. They not only melt you, but they also motivate you. If they can pass through the trials of life, so can you.

EXTREME PERSONAL LESSON:

On life's highway, God will place near you those who have had experiences similar to yours. Listen to them. These seasoned saints can help guide you down the path of life.

It's so true. Problems in life oftentimes come barreling down our highway like a driver on the wrong side of the road. We spend countless waking hours just trying to make it safely to our destination. Just when things seem to be back on track and we're again making progress, WHAM! Here comes another hit from hell. We lose our job. The doctor informs us we're terminally ill. Our child is hurt or killed in an accident. Our home burns down. A tornado sweeps through our town. A terrorist attack kills a friend or relative. Whatever it may be, we're left crying out, "God, how could You allow this to happen! Why?!"

Friend, we have so many lessons to learn. Many of these lessons are best taught by God through difficulties. He teaches us to trust Him by allowing us to go through a financial trial. He teaches us to pray for others by allowing us to feel some of their pain.

He lets us experience struggles so we can have practical wisdom to help others. The comforting counsel others receive from us during their trials is a direct result of the comfort we received from God during ours.

Paul was no stranger to trials and assures us that "the Father of mercies and God of all comfort" will comfort us in "all our affliction so that we may be able to comfort those who are in any affliction with the comfort with which we ourselves are comforted by God" (2 Cor. 1:3-4).

EXTREME PERSONAL LESSON:

Many of our struggles have a purpose that extends far past the boundaries of our lives. God lends us a hand during our time of need, so we can lend a hand to others when they're in need.

My first major trial came as a shock, not only to me but also to my family. Several weeks had passed since that historic October 1975 morning when Jesus washed me clean. Soon after receiving Christ as my Savior, I got involved at my mom's church in Huntsville, eventually training with the puppet ministry for kids. The Lord was working in my life, and although my spiritual growth was slow, it was real.

One night, about midnight, the doorbell rang. Mom answered the door and found two uniformed deputies and a plainclothes narcotics agent standing on our front porch. The agent made the reason for their visit clear: "Ma'am, we're here to arrest Stephen Hill for felonies he committed against the state of Alabama. Is he here?" These all too familiar words cut like a knife in my mom's spirit. I had been arrested so many times before. Now, just a few weeks into my Christian life, I once again was being arrested.

Mom had no choice but to let them in. "He's in the back bedroom, officers, but he's different now. He's no longer involved in drugs and crime. He's a Christian."

"Yes, ma'am, we understand," one of the officers said, as they made their way to my room. They had heard that one before.

I can't imagine what Mom was going through. She had been there when her drug-crazed son was miraculously transformed from a criminal into a Christian, when the face of a hardened young man changed into the countenance of an innocent child.

I was lying on my bed watching a late-night talk show when the narcotics agent knocked. He didn't wait for my permission to enter—this was a drug bust. The door swung open, and I knew what was happening. There had been rumors around town of a major crackdown. My friends and I had been actively involved in selling large quantities of hard narcotics. We had made a lot of money and had consumed a lot of drugs—it had been a wild year. Now the wages of sin were coming down hard.

The narcotics agent, flanked by the two armed officers, came up to me and said, "Don't move, Steve. The house is surrounded." I lay motionless. He pulled from his pocket four envelopes. His words sent shivers through my soul. "Steve, each of these envelopes contains a felony warrant for your arrest. One of these warrants represents a maximum of 25 years in the state pen. I have four. If three of them don't stick, one will. We have you for at least 25 years. Now get dressed, you're coming with us."

I was cuffed and escorted past my mom who was waiting in the living room—the moment is etched in my mind forever. I turned to her and said, "It's gonna' be all right, Mom. Don't worry. Everything's going to work out." Little did I know that this arrest marked the pivotal point to my Christian walk and that jail would be the launch pad for the most phenomenal years of my life.

A few minutes later I arrived at the Madison County jail in downtown Huntsville. The local media was out in full force; the TV cameras were rolling. This was a big bust—a great story!

They stuffed the few possessions I had on me in a paper bag and labeled it "Property of inmate Stephen Hill." A Polaroid camera took my mug shot. You could tell the wardens on duty were tired—it had been a long and busy night. Their cache of photos contained the "who's who" of the local drug scene.

A plaque with my name, number and the date was placed in my hands. It was about two o'clock in the morning as the flash lit up the room. Next was the all-too-familiar fingerprinting process. I knew the steps by heart. I remember thinking to myself, *Where is this going to end? I'll probably end up with my many friends already doing hard time in prison.* But God had a plan.

The jail was jammed to capacity and tempers were boiling over. Local law enforcement had successfully rounded up most of the dealers in town. Suspicion was sweeping the cells. Everyone knew that someone had infiltrated our drug scene—but who?

Many of the inmates were violent criminals who had an insatiable thirst for blood. They wanted vengeance. Who would be the target? Would it be the guy sleeping in the bunk above me or would I be chosen as their object of wrath? Would it be the new guy arrested last night? The police often threw one of their own in jail to eavesdrop on our conversations. These narcs knew how to talk the talk and walk the walk, so we had no way of knowing.

I decided to keep a journal to break up the monotony of the long days. Fights were constantly breaking out. Inmates were beaten up by other inmates for no reason, and cruel stunts were pulled simply for entertainment. I recorded some of them in my journal:

Tommy pulled a dirty trick on Roger today. Tommy was on the top bunk, pretending to be asleep while his buddy, Cherokee, told Roger to tie a string around Tommy's foot and light it. As soon as Roger lit the match, Tommy jumped up and nailed him bad. What a jerk. It was hilarious to everybody but Roger. He was an idiot to fall for it.

Mail call came every day. Family and Christian friends faithfully sent notes, cards and letters of encouragement. I received some letters from an anonymous Christian who called herself the Pink Seal, because each letter was sealed with her trademark drop of pink wax. Her letters came on a regular basis and lifted me up during some of my darkest days. I still don't know her identity, but I thank God she had a burden for my soul.

EXTREME PERSONAL LESSON:

Random acts of kindness may seem simple here on earth, but their value and effect are recorded in heaven. An act of love to a suffering brother or sister can rejuvenate the spirit. Make it a habit to reach out.

My favorite time was Sundays when preachers, all makes and models, came to the jail to scream at us about Jesus. Some would preach so hard and so loud that their neck veins bulged and their faces turned beet-red. It was fascinating, and an honor, to be in their captive audience. During previous seasons of incarceration I had mocked and made fun of their labor of love. Now, as a new Christian, I was ready to learn.

One group of ministers had a burden to teach us the Word of God through written Bible lessons. Each Sunday they would give us a homework assignment for the week. Those of us who cared completed the studies by the following Sunday and turned them in. I received a diploma after successfully completing six weeks of lessons. It felt good.

EXTREME PERSONAL LESSON:

Like Paul and Silas, who sang praises in prison, look for the good during dark and discouraging times.

Finally, things were starting to look up. A visit by Rev. Jim Summers from the Huntsville-based Outreach Ministries, was a good indicator of better times to come. Jim's program is affiliated with the Teen Challenge program founded by David Wilkerson. Both programs help troubled young men and women grow in their knowledge of Christ and get their lives on track.

Jim worked closely with the court system and often was able to offer his ministry as an alternative to prison. My name was being bounced around as a possibility for the Outreach Ministries Teen Challenge program. From the beginning, the judge made it clear he was against it; still, he was considering giving me one more chance. God had a plan.

I spent Christmas, New Year's Day and my twenty-second birthday in jail. By February 1976 my day in court had finally arrived. I was cuffed and led down to a holding cell outside the courtroom. Just a few feet away were the judge's chambers. He had the power to release me to Teen Challenge or send me to prison for many years. My prayer was simple. "Jesus, please take control of this situation. I need You."

A deputy escorted me into the courtroom and to my seat. As the judge entered, the bailiff's booming voice announced, "All rise!"

Out of the many court cases that day, mine was first. A decision had already been made: I was to plead guilty and rest my fate in the hands of the judge. The bailiff read from the day's docket, "The state of Alabama verses Stephen L. Hill." My lawyer and I approached the bench. The judge was quick to let me know of his mistrust of my character—I was more than a three-time loser and deserved to be incarcerated. I was a menace to society.

He then made a statement that changed my destiny. "Stephen Hill, this is against my better judgment, but I'm going to probate you to Jim Summers and Outreach Ministries of Alabama. If you don't successfully complete this program, if you so much as break one rule, you'll be sent to the state penitentiary. Next case!"

Within minutes, it was all over. Freedom was just a few steps away. The paperwork was completed and the big brass key turned the tumblers in the lock for the last time. The paper bag containing my possessions was turned upside down and the contents dumped on the counter; I scooped them up and walked out the door. A van was waiting to escort me to my new home. The trip took only 20 minutes, but it was enough time to ponder the events of the past several months. From drug addiction to conversion to jail, then on to Outreach Ministries. God knew I would have never entered this program without His intervention. What looked like the end of my life turned out to be the work of His guiding hand. What an amazing, loving God we serve!

EXTREME PERSONAL LESSON:

Negative circumstances often bring about positive results. When confronted with adverse situations, always remember that all things—not just some things—work together for good.

On my first night out of jail and in the Teen Challenge program, the Outreach van was loaded up and all of us remanded convicts were taken to a revival meeting at a nearby church. The worship was out of this world—people were clapping and singing. About an hour into the service, an evangelist stepped up to the pulpit, opened his Bible and read Job 19:25: "And as for me, I know that my Redeemer lives."

Job knew all about trials and knew whom to trust. The significance of hearing that particular verse on that day was not lost on me and tears flowed down my face. I had just been delivered from years in prison—I was free, both physically and spiritually.

After the service, folks came over and warmly welcomed me to the church. I looked pretty rough—my hair was long and scraggly, I sported a full beard, but nobody cared. As a matter of fact, several weeks later the young pastor asked me to play Jesus in the church's Easter play—he said I looked the part. The congregation's genuine Christian love and affection were overwhelming.

EXTREME PERSONAL LESSON:

Don't judge based upon outward appearances. God sees the heart. Give the Holy Spirit time to change people into the image of Christ.

It was time for me to grow, and soon lessons began coming my way at an unbelievable rate. God had His hand on my life and was determined to chip off the rough exterior in order to transform my mind with His Word and make me into a true man of God. The first area to be dealt with was my deceitful character. God would make me honest and His plan was perfect.

As His Word was going in, the garbage of the world was coming out. Psalm 119:9 (*NKJV*) puts it this way, "How can a young man cleanse his way? By taking heed according to Your word."

In my first week at the Outreach Ministries Teen Challenge home, I was elected cook. It was a landslide victory—but not an honor. Nobody wanted the position, and it usually fell to the low man on the totem pole—and at the time that was me. My duties were to rise early, whip up some breakfast, feed the famished, clean up and then repeat the process for lunch and dinner. Sometimes I had help, but normally I carried out these duties alone.

A large sack of flour was donated to the ministry, presenting the exciting possibility of creating the guys' all-time favorite breakfast: biscuits and gravy (hey, we were in Alabama!). There was just one problem. The flour contained thousands of little, black-pepper-looking specks. Upon close examination I discovered each speck had legs and could move. Yes, my friend, our donation was riddled with bugs.

A decision had to be made. There was absolutely no way to separate the good from the bad, so I called the men together for a vote. "All in favor of biscuits with bugs, raise your hand." It was unanimous. A new culinary creation would be introduced to these new creations in Christ. After all, what's a few little bugs? They looked like pepper and might even add a meaty flavor.

The next day I rose early, prepared enough biscuits to feed a small army, piled them on the plates, drenched them in gravy and summoned the men to breakfast. It was almost embarrassing the way they ate. Proper etiquette was foreign to these famished souls. Anyone from polished, high society would have run for cover. Within minutes the plates were licked spotless and the satisfied savages went on their way. I was left to clean up.

In all the excitement and flurry of preparation, I forgot to take time to eat my own breakfast. There remained on the stove two lonely biscuits that represented all that was left of this bountiful breakfast. I reached over, grabbed one and, without even thinking, chomped into it. Then something happened that absolutely blew my mind. The conviction of the Holy Spirit swept through me like a river. You see, there was a house rule, simple and clear: No eating between meals. Breakfast was over. I was breaking the rule.

"But, God," I complained, "I'm the cook. I prepared the breakfast. It's my right to eat the food." Of course, there was truth to my statement. But I knew that a rule had been broken. The deep, gut-wrenching feeling wouldn't go away.

I couldn't believe what was happening. This former drug addict, this felon, this thief who had once stolen anything he wanted was now falling under conviction for eating a biscuit. Not robbing a bank, not grand theft auto, not some major drug deal—I felt horrible for sticking a bug-infested biscuit in my mouth.

Remember, nobody saw me commit the crime—well, nobody human, that is. The fact remains that there are always three witnesses to every crime and every sin: the Father, the Son and the Holy Ghost.

Depression flooded me. My joy was gone. I couldn't even sing in chapel. The young man who was always "up" was now always "down." This went on for days and eventually weeks. Finally, the pressure was too great, and it was time for confession.

Early one morning I saw the head staff member walk into

the house, and I heard the Lord tell me, "It's time to confess, Steve." With head hung down, I pulled him aside, "Brother, I need to talk to you."

"Sure, Steve," he said. "Step into my office." The moment of truth had come.

He had noticed my drastic mood change. I had gone from cheerful Christian to guilty child. The other staff members knew something was wrong, but they were waiting patiently for the right time to help. He sat behind his desk and braced himself for the worst. Had I committed a murder and concealed it? Slipped out at night and gotten drunk? Was there a stash of drugs under my mattress? What would this former criminal-turned-Christian confess?

Looking like a whipped pup, I poured out my heart and did not withhold a single detail. I explained that after the meal was over, I had been dutifully cleaning up the dishes. Hoping to solicit some sympathy, I described how I had been laboring over this meal for a couple of hours and had forgotten to eat. Two biscuits remained on the stove and, without even thinking, I reached over and grabbed one.

By this time, my heart was beating rapidly. It was as if I were surrounded by darkness and a bright light was shining into my face. It was the moment of truth. Sweat began forming on my palms. And then, bursting into a heart-rending confession, I blurted out, "Brother, I ate it! I ate the biscuit! Please, please forgive me!"

He sat silent with both hands cupped over his mouth, attempting to hide a smile. A burst of laughter almost escaped, but he held back. He was prepared for bank robbery, not biscuit robbery.

Beyond the humor of the story, he knew sitting before him was a young man learning the importance of sensitivity to God. The Holy Ghost had convicted me of something small, and I was yielding. This was the making of a true man of God, and he knew it.

"Steve, I forgive you," he said. "But you still broke a rule in this program. We have rules to keep order. You have spent your life running from responsibility and in absolute rebellion against authority. Now, as a Christian, you are being taught some valuable lessons by God. As punishment, I want you to scrub every speck of dirt off the kitchen floor."

He led me into the kitchen. Under the sink was a small brush, like the ones used to clean fingernails. Then he continued, "Get on your hands and knees and clean every square inch of this kitchen—behind the stove, the refrigerator, everywhere. I hope this serves as a lesson to you. Disobedience to God carries consequences."

I grabbed the brush, got a pail of soapy water and began scrubbing. Just a few months earlier, I would have cleaned out every freshly baked donut from the corner Krispy Kreme without any remorse. Now I was submitting to punishment for stealing a biscuit. What more proof did anyone need to see that Jesus was changing my life?

The work was grueling and tedious, but my heart and spirit were free. As I circled around the kitchen with that tiny brush, the Holy Spirit whispered these words: "Steve, if you will be faithful in the small things, I will bless you with larger things. Keep your conscience clear. Stay sensitive to Me." I felt the warm smile of God.

EXTREME PERSONAL LESSON:

Sensitivity to the Holy Spirit is an absolute requirement for anyone wishing to become a servant of God. Learn to be obedient in everything. The smallest sin to man is great in God's eyes. He's not looking for sacrifice as much as obedience.

To this day, I still have that sensitivity. Little things bother me; I abhor anything that drifts into the realm of disobedience. Why? Because I seek God's favor. Acts 24:16 says we're "to maintain always a blameless conscience both before God and before men."

Let me ask you a few questions. Why should God bless anyone with more money if she is not faithful to tithe on what she already has? Why should God give one of His children more earthly possessions if he is not a faithful steward over what he already possesses? If we can't be trusted in small things, why should God bless us with larger things? Just like an earthly father is grieved by his child's "little white lie," so our heavenly Father is grieved when we choose to disobey—even in little things.

I challenge you with this: If there's anything you've done to grieve the Lord, repent and get right with Him! If you need to go to another brother or sister to make things right, do it! Remember, sin separates us from God. It puts a ceiling of brass between God and us. Learn the joy of living under an open heaven.

But, Steve, you may be thinking, *you're talking about radical change. You're talking about becoming sold-out to holiness and righteous living.* That's right, friend—get serious with God. Remember, if you get serious with God, He'll get serious with you. I challenge you to be one of those who dare to follow Christ completely.

Learnin' to Love

CHAPTER THREE

EXTREME LESSON:

Throughout our Christian lives, God allows us to come in contact with others whose personalities force us to demonstrate the love of Jesus.

"By this all men will know that you are My disciples, if you have love for one another."

JOHN 13:35

Receiving the love of Jesus by accepting Him as

Savior is one thing. Learning to love others is quite another. As I begin writing this chapter, I feel that I'm entering shark-infested waters. The devil and all his demons would love for you to stop reading right now. If he could just keep you from forming friendships; if he could successfully drive a wedge between you and your brother; if he could put in your mind a suspicious thought or craft a little lie that would pull you away from your sister; if he could keep each strand from braiding together into that unbreakable rope, then he would succeed. That's why you must read on.

The fact that brethren within the Church Body don't get along must grieve our heavenly Father and cause deep pain in the heart of Christ. The Holy Spirit works overtime wooing us to one another in an attempt to heal our relationships and bind up our wounded spirits. He wants us to be friends. Only God knows how many churches have split over petty differences. A little ripple in their relationships with each other, and you'd think they were broadsided by a tidal wave. As Christians depart in defeat, the devil and his imps parade through hell on their victory float declaring, "We won! We divided the brethren! They don't trust each other anymore."

Why are we surprised? The devil is just doing what he does best. Revelation 12:10 says, "And I heard a loud voice saying in heaven, 'Now the salvation, and the power, and the kingdom of our God and the authority of His Christ have come, for the accuser of our brethren has been thrown down, who accuses them before our God day and night.'"

Don't you get it? His role is that of a deceiver, a liar and accuser. Over 30 times in the Bible we find him associated with the word "accuser." That's what he does. And if he's gonna spew his poison toward God in heaven, don't you think he's going to spew it down here toward us on earth?

I remember evangelizing in a neighborhood in a midwest town. Every encounter was unique, but one remains etched on my mind to this day.

At one home, a man answered his door and barked out through the screen, "Who are you and whadd'ya want?" My reply was simple: "My name is Steve Hill, and I'm holding a revival at the church down the street. I want you to know that Jesus loves you and has a plan for your life. We'd love for you to come join us."

With that he started cussing, beer in one hand and a lit cigarette in the other, "You couldn't pay me to attend that *blankety-blank* church! I used to be a member there! As a matter of fact, I was on the committee that helped build the facility you're preaching in!"

He was so consumed with anger that I thought he'd start foaming at the mouth. The plot continued to thicken and by now he was almost breathing fire: "We had to purchase all kinds of materials. I told the committee members that my brother owned a brick factory on the other side of town. When it came time to purchase bricks for the sanctuary, I told the pastor I'd get him a good deal. The pastor visited the factory, but he decided to get the bricks from another company—even though I had already told my brother it was a done deal. The pastor made a fool outta me, so I pulled him aside one day, gave him a piece of my mind and stomped out of the church. That was five years ago. You couldn't pay me to return to that church."

I almost said, "Don't worry, Bubba. Ain't no one gonna offer you a plug nickel to come back," but I restrained myself.

My actual response shocked him: "Sir, are you telling me that you fell away from God and fellowship with your Christian friends because of *building materials*? My friend, don't go to hell over a load of bricks." With that he mumbled a few choice words and slammed the door in my face.

EXTREME PERSONAL LESSON:

Don't allow a little disagreement to turn into a monumental problem. Don't shut out your brothers and sisters in Christ just because they don't see things your way.

You're probably thinking that this man overreacted, but if the truth be known, people have left churches over much less. Rather than demonstrate the love, patience and kindness of Christ, they've yielded to the enemy and gotten spiritually shipwrecked over some petty issue.

Friend, we must learn to love. We must work out our differences under the guidance of the Holy Spirit and learn to forgive: "And whenever you stand praying, forgive, if you have anything against anyone; so that your Father also who is in heaven may forgive you your transgressions. But if you do not forgive, neither will your Father who is in heaven forgive your trespasses" (Mark 11:25-26). Learning to forgive is a lesson I learned early on in my Christian walk. It was a lesson forced on me by Jesus when I was just a baby Christian. During that time in my life I was in constant warfare with the old nature.

I came out of the drug culture and street life where unfamiliar people were discarded like trash and everyone was a potential enemy. Hate, suspicion and paranoia characterized our culture. In contrast, as a newborn child of God, I was learning about the love and compassion of Jesus. I was hearing and reading God's Word, and it was changing my life. I could really relate to Paul's words: "Therefore if any man is in Christ, he is a new creature; the old things passed away; behold, new things have come" (2 Cor. 5:17).

My heart of stone was becoming a heart of flesh. Ezekiel 11:19-20 puts it this way: "And I shall give them one heart, and shall put a new spirit within them. And I shall take the heart of stone out of their flesh and give them a heart of flesh, that they may walk in My statutes and keep My ordinances, and do them. Then they will be My people, and I shall be their God."

My old selfish thought patterns were being pierced by the sword of the Spirit. God was doing some deep excavation and coming up with some serious junk. He wanted me to learn about love and He wanted me to learn right there and then!

Outreach Ministries and Teen Challenge run very structured programs. New students voluntarily give up what many would consider their personal rights. I had to memorize pages of rules—even the rules had rules. Just to give you an idea: Personal showers were limited to five minutes; no eating between meals was allowed (remember the biscuit?); students were not permitted to speak to one another unless a staff member was present (to avoid the possibility of guys boasting about their street exploits); and so on.

Every student was guaranteed "three hots and a cot"—three meals and a bed. There were two bunk beds in each room, and we could not choose our roommates. I had been in the program about six weeks when God decided to test my new people skills. My test came in the form of Billy, a scrawny 13-year-old kid with a Woody Woodpecker laugh and an annoying personality. The average age in the program was about 25, so for a young minor to be admitted into the home was very unusual—I thought for sure there was a rule against it, especially considering *this* kid. But God had a plan.

Billy was assigned to the bottom bed in my bunk, and he became an immediate irritant to me. His favorite pastime was placing his feet directly under the center of my bunk and kicking.

I would look at him over the edge of my bunk and warn of impending doom, but Billy would only laugh. I couldn't hit him—it was against the rules. No one liked Billy. He was a nuisance, and we avoided him like the plague but to no avail. Where do you go, where do you hide when there are 17 guys living in a four-bedroom, two-story house?

EXTREME PERSONAL LESSON:

The Bible says that all things work together for good. You've been placed where you are by God for a purpose. Don't run from the lesson to be learned.

Finally, after enduring two weeks of nerve-grating torment from Dennis the Menace, I had to get help. I went to the staff pleading for a reprieve. Little did I know, Billy had already been to the staff—he was fed up with me! My leader's response was simple yet extremely difficult to swallow. But it was advice I would end up sharing for years to come in my own ministry. He said, "Get along with Billy. Spend time with him. Ask Jesus to help you find his good characteristics." The leader told me to read Philippians 2:3-8, so I went back to my room (thankfully no one was there) and read the passage:

Do nothing from selfishness or empty conceit, but with humility of mind *let each of you regard one another as more important than himself; do not merely look out for your own personal interests, but also for the interests of others.* Have this attitude in yourselves which was also in Christ Jesus, who, although He existed in the form of God, did not

regard equality with God a thing to be grasped, but emp-
tied Himself, taking the form of a bond-servant, and
being made in the likeness of men. And being found in
the appearance as a man, He humbled Himself by
becoming obedient to the point of death, even death on
a cross (emphasis added).

It nailed me. I was overcome with conviction and determined to follow Paul's advice. It would end up changing my life.

One of the upstairs rooms had been turned into a library,
and that's where I found Billy later that day. He had a box of colored pencils and was busy drawing when I swung open the door.
Mustering up all the sincerity I could, I asked, "Hey, Billy,
what'cha doin'?"

He replied, "Just drawing some cartoons, that's all."

"Can I see?"

"Sure, why not."

I was shocked—this young kid handed me some of the most
professional cartoon art I had ever seen. In a bewildered voice I
said, "You drew this?"

"Sure," he said, "that's what I do. I'm a professional car-
toonist. My comics have even been published. Look, I'll show
you a few." Looking over his work, all I could say was, "Man,
Billy, you're good—really good."

It was like a cloud lifted from the room. There was now a
connection between us. I pulled up a chair and began talking
with Billy and discovered that underneath the giddy exterior was
a fascinating human being, blessed with God-given talent. In the
past I had done some work as a graphic artist, so over the next
few days and weeks Billy and I pooled our talents.

The staff gave us permission to make illustrated Scripture
posters. I would ink the words, such as "The good man eats to
live, while the evil man lives to eat" (Prov. 13:25, *TLB*); and Billy

would fill the poster with caricatures of the students. Around this particular Scripture text, Billy drew cartoons of our students slopping like pigs at a trough. Our efforts paid off. We hung that one in the kitchen, and the guys began eating in a more civilized manner.

Billy and I became best friends. We prayed and read the Bible together. Although he still had his childish ways about him, things were different now. We were brothers in the Lord, so we looked past each other's faults. We no longer majored on minors.

I was learning to apply the teaching from the Sermon on the Mount when Jesus said, "And why do you look at the speck that is in your brother's eye, but do not notice the log that is in your own eye? Or how can you say to your brother, 'Let me take the speck out of your eye,' and behold, the log is in your own eye? You hypocrite, first take the log out of your own eye, and then you will see clearly to take the speck out of your brother's eye" (Matt. 7:3-5).

Billy and I were living out this Scripture and a wonderful friendship developed.

EXTREME PERSONAL LESSON:

We are all members of the Body of Christ. If you are offended by a brother, go to that person and work it out. Perhaps he too has been offended or hurt by you.

The Teen Challenge program is divided into different phases. The first phase in Alabama lasted three months and I had completed it. I then moved to the second phase, at a Teen Challenge home in Cape Girardeau, Missouri, where I would spend the next 10 months in intense Bible training. Under the watchful eye of Director Herb Meppelink, this program had produced hundreds of on-fire graduates.

Billy, who was back in Alabama, became lonely after I, who was basically his only friend, moved away. The other guys had not been interested in his artwork and began poking fun at him. The pressure was too much, and late one night he slipped away and hitchhiked back home to Chicago.

It was early one morning in Missouri when I received a phone call from Jim Summers in Alabama, "Steve, I've got some very sad news. Billy was murdered."

I couldn't believe my ears. Surely it was just a bad joke. But Jim went on to explain how Billy had been treated by the others after I had left, how he then ran away one night and headed for home. "When he arrived," Jim said, "his house was ambushed by a gang and Billy was killed. I'm sorry, Steve. We loved Billy very much."

I then found out that Billy had been an eyewitness to a mafia-type murder. He was the only link to the killer and had agreed to testify at the trial. He was staying at the Teen Challenge home in hiding, waiting for the trial to begin. With Billy dead, the killer would be exonerated. But much worse was that now my friend, my little brother in the Lord, was dead. Tears welled up as I thought of the love between two brothers. After wiping my eyes, I got on my knees and thanked God for teaching me how to love.

EXTREME PERSONAL LESSON:

Don't let the sun go down on your anger. Learn to love and show your love while you have the opportunity. There may come a day when it's too late.

The result of my spending time with Billy was a friendship so deep that even today I shudder at what my life would have been like without him. God was determined to make me and mold me into the image of Jesus. He was going to purposely put me with others who would shape the character of Jesus in my life.

As Christians, all of us must learn to die to self. Our flesh has received a death sentence from God. Paul put it like this, "I have been crucified with Christ; and it is no longer I who live, but Christ lives in me; and the life which I now live in the flesh I live by faith in the Son of God, who loved me, and delivered Himself up for me" (Gal. 2:20).

You cannot crucify yourself—you need help. You can nail your feet, reach over and nail one hand, but who is going to nail your other hand? Billy helped me and I helped him—we helped each other to crucify our carnal natures.

My brothers and sisters: Love the brethren. It's a powerful lesson for those who dare to obey Christ completely.

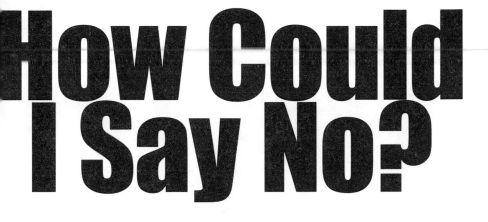

How Could I Say No?

CHAPTER FOUR

EXTREME LESSON:

If we pursue the Lord and His will for our lives, He will provide the things we need.

"But seek first His kingdom and His righteousness;
and all these things shall be added to you."

MATTHEW 6:33

I finished up the 13-month program in 1977, so with my Teen Challenge diploma in hand, I had to make a career decision. What did I want to do? Was secular employment the next step or should I pursue ministry? How could I discern if God wanted me in the ministry or if it was just my own personal dream? The answer was clear.

You see, there is a great danger here. Many people who are called to work for God become too spiritually minded and they miss the simplicity of the call. They desire three dreams and a vision about their future, when God has chosen to speak to them in a still, small voice. They want a new revelation from heaven, while God has already given them a clear commission on earth.

Like those investigating the possibility of military enlistment, they want to hear about all the benefits, while God is waiting for them to sign on the dotted line. They ask the question, "Where will You take me?" God responds with a five-word statement, "Go into all the world." They want celestial signs, but God wants serious soldiers.

For me, there was a deep ever-present desire in my spirit to do something for God. I wanted to win people to Jesus and see them grow as I had grown. That was enough for me. That was enough for God. I had been called. Now what?

EXTREME PERSONAL LESSON:

Don't be quick to exclude yourself from the call of God. Your appetite for souls may be evidence of a deep calling on your life.

The Bible is full of guidance promises. Look at Proverbs 3:5-6, "Trust in the LORD with all your heart, and do not lean on your own understanding. In all your ways acknowledge Him, and He will make your paths straight."

Or consider Philippians 1:6: "For I am confident of this very thing, that He who began a good work in you will perfect it until the day of Christ Jesus." To me this verse said in plain simple terms that God had made a new person out of me and He was going to continue His work.

Now that I was a Teen Challenge graduate, Outreach Ministries invited me back to Huntsville to join them as a junior staff member. I accepted. What a joy it was to share with new students how God would work in their lives if they'd just obey. I was busy and content working for God. Weeks turned into months, and I was having the time of my life serving in the ministry.

Just think of it. Jesus had taken a rebellious, confused drug addict, saved him, transformed him and was now using him to help others. What a miracle! The pay wasn't much, but that didn't matter. The work was rewarding, and I was moving forward with God.

I often say it's a whole lot easier to steer a moving car than one that's sitting still. Many people just sit around waiting for their marching orders. I say to them, "Get going! Do something! Involve yourself in ministry. Clean up trash around the church. Scrape the chewing gum off the bottom of church pews." Remember, God is looking for motivated people.

EXTREME PERSONAL LESSON:

Find something to do for God, and do it with all your might. Stay busy for Jesus. No task is too menial when it's done for Him.

Several months into my new assignment, an opportunity came that would change my life forever. David Wilkerson had recently opened Twin Oaks Academy, a Bible school in Lindale, Texas. His desire was to find 50 serious men and women from across the country, bring them to the academy, train them for ministry and then send them out. I had been chosen to attend and accepted the assignment without any hesitation.

What a dream come true! The new campus was located in beautiful countryside on a sprawling 400-acre ranch in East Texas. Wilkerson always did everything first-class for God, and this campus proved to be better than what I had imagined. We had spacious men's and women's dormitories separated by gorgeous landscaping. A small Old West-style town sat atop a hill overlooking the dorms and connecting all the buildings was a wooden boardwalk. Along the meandering boardwalk were the classrooms, library, laundry facilities, barbershop, medical clinic, small hotel, gymnasium and cafeteria. Several lakes divided up the property and thousands of trees dotted the landscape.

It was heaven on earth for this ex-drug addict who wanted to enter full-time ministry. The ranch was like a spiritual oasis, a paradise for prayer—and that's what I did. This was the opportunity of a lifetime that had to be seized during the lifetime of the opportunity.

We're all creatures of routine and I quickly entered mine. I got up every morning around four o'clock, strapped on my running shoes, put in a mile and then returned to my dorm room to pray. What a glorious time of prayer that was! All alone, at the breaking of day, I would bombard heaven with petitions for others and desires of my own. And Jesus was there.

A roommate ridiculed me for rising early to go after God. That's right—a Bible school student harassing me for my Christian fervor. Go figure. I realized at the time it was probably jealousy or conviction and I ignored his cutting words.

EXTREME PERSONAL LESSON:

Go after God regardless of the opinions of others. You came into this world alone, and you'll leave alone. You're responsible for your own spirituality.

Along the way, I've learned firsthand why the Bible says, "So then, my beloved, just as you have always obeyed, not as in my presence only, but now much more in my absence, work out your salvation with fear and trembling" (Phil. 2:12).

The academic sessions were held in the morning. Special visiting speakers such as Nicky Cruz, a former gang leader featured in Wilkerson's book, taught on evangelism, and revivalist Leonard Ravenhill taught on prayer. Other quality professors took us deep into the Word of God.

Singer and songwriter Dallas Holm and his band sang at our weekly prayer meetings; David Wilkerson preached; and singer and songwriter Keith Green lived nearby and often joined us for lunch. He gave free concerts at the neighboring Agape Force ranch.

We students often felt like life on the campus was too good to be true. The best of the best was surrounding us. Later we learned that we would be held accountable to God for all He had given us.

Tim and LaDonna Johnson, formerly with country singer Tammy Wynette's band, had gotten serious about God and were now part of Dallas Holm's band. This dynamic couple also formed a music ensemble with a dozen students. When they weren't touring, they would take us to churches for ministry. What an awesome season of practical training!

Not only were we well-trained academically, but we were also expected to take this knowledge to the next level. We were taught homiletics (sermon preparation and preaching) and then required to apply this knowledge by preparing a sermon. Many students who felt a call to preach were granted permission to speak at our Thursday night services.

I'll never forget the feeling I had when a staff member informed me that my time to preach had come. Knowing that world-renowned evangelist and Bible expositor David Wilkerson would possibly be in the congregation made sermon preparation an agonizing task. He knew the Bible a lot; I knew the Bible a little. He was a great saint; I was a green student. He was a prolific writer; I was a petrified writer. He had fire; I had fear. He had hundreds of powerful sermons; I had none. Still, I went to the school library for some guidance and inspiration. The Lord had laid a thought on my mind about the little foxes that spoil the vine found in the Song of Solomon 2:15, "Catch the foxes for us, the little foxes that are ruining the vineyards, while our vineyards are in blossom."

Was I to prepare a message on the fox? Was I to preach about the little sins that creep into our lives and destroy the fruit of our vineyard? Was this God or Steve? Something then happened that motivated me to not only prepare the message but also to deliver it under the unction of the Holy Ghost.

While reaching up to pull down a book from the top shelf, a small square piece of paper fell out and floated to the floor. I watched it drift back and forth and eventually settle by my feet. Reaching down to pick it up, I was stunned by what I saw: a color picture of a little red fox running through a meadow. My immediate words were, "Thank You, Jesus."

God was reaching down and saying to this young, unprepared, scared little child, "I'm with you, son. Here's a simple sign just to show you how close I am." When my night to preach arrived, David Wilkerson was unable to make it, but many from his crusade team and all the students were present. I preached with boldness and many responded to the altar call. I knew in my heart that God had given me this message.

EXTREME PERSONAL LESSON:

We are children of God. Just as God sent a raven to feed Elijah when he felt all alone, God will often send us a sign just to show us He is near. Although these times may be rare, learn to recognize the ravens and thank Him for them.

Each afternoon the students were required to work around the property doing various chores. Since Wilkerson's ministry was paying our tuition, room and board, no one complained about the afternoon job assignments.

My job involved driving a small, orange Datsun pick-up truck to carry out my duties as the ministry gopher. Each afternoon I would drive into Dallas or Tyler to pick up supplies and deliver them to the respective departments. I would "go for" this and "go for" that but before taking off, I'd check in with each department to find out what they needed.

In one department there was a student working as a receptionist. She loved Jesus and was cute—my top two requirements in my prayers for a wife. She had a smile that could change your day and a voice that made me want to stay. Her name was Jeri. My name was Mush.

I couldn't believe this was happening. How could this woman cause a dedicated, serious prayer warrior to stumble over his words like a bumbling fool? Easy. It was the love bug and I'd been bitten.

I prayed, oh, how I prayed. Every morning the heavens heard me. "Thank You, Jesus, for sending Jeri into my life. Now, Lord, help! What do I do next? Guide me, Lord Jesus!" Little did I know Jeri was also rising early to pray, but her prayer was quite different: "Dear Jesus, take this man out of my life. I don't want a relationship with anyone but You. Take away these feelings I have for him."

Of course, everyone knows whose prayers Jesus listened to and answered. Jeri's requests for the relationship to grind to a halt were short-circuited by my prayers for it to move full-speed ahead.

But we had one small problem. Wilkerson's Twin Oaks Academy, like Teen Challenge, had serious rules about dating—it was to be nonexistent. No relationships with members of the opposite sex were allowed. The school wanted its students to focus on their spiritual growth and didn't want anything distracting us from moving forward with God.

As time moved on, our love began to grow. (My prayers were being answered!) There was only one thing to do. Jeri and I met with the staff and shared our dilemma. To our amazement, they understood.

We were quickly given strict guidelines. We could speak to each other for only 15 minutes a day. We could not sit together in church or the cafeteria. We could not hold hands, and there was to be absolutely no "PDA" (you know, public or private displays of affection). The staff was convinced that if our relationship was of God, then He would bring it to fruition.

EXTREME PERSONAL LESSON:

Boundaries are given by God to protect us. Don't reject godly counsel that asks you to restrain from personal desires. This may be protecting you from imminent danger.

Counsel also came from everyone else—some was encouraging, some was not. One day Gwen Wilkerson, David's wife, was cutting my hair in the boardwalk barber shop. This was one of her hobbies, and I never passed up a free haircut. (She later was instrumental in teaching Jeri how to cut hair, and to this day I've never paid for a haircut!) With scissors in one hand and a comb in the other, Gwen began clipping my locks.

I've always respected Gwen's gift of discernment but, nevertheless, was taken aback when she sweetly but boldly declared, "You know, Steve. You might be missing God in this. Jeri may not be the girl for you. It may be a mistake you'll live to regret."

This wasn't exactly what I wanted to hear, but I understood where Gwen was coming from. She realized the suffocating power of infatuation and feared I might not be thinking rationally. She had seen many young men and women fall in love, marry in haste and then a few years down the road pass through a heart-wrenching divorce. Her words were a warning and helped keep me firmly grounded. I cautiously moved forward. Besides, never argue with someone who's cutting your hair!

EXTREME PERSONAL LESSON:

Listen to the opinion of those you respect, even when their opinion is contrary to yours. Their words, when fitly spoken, can help keep your feet on solid ground.

Several months had gone by and Jeri and I were deeply in love. We knew we were meant for one other, even though we hadn't been out on a date, hadn't held hands, had never kissed. Thanks to the rigid rules, we had spent far more time praying than playing. But I couldn't stand it anymore—it was time to ask her to marry me.

I was broke, so there was no money to buy a ring. The strict guidelines at the school ruled out any kind of romantic dinner, lakeside picnic or even a midnight cruise in the orange Datsun pickup. What was I to do? I only had our 15-minute meeting time to pop the most important question of my life.

To anybody who might be thinking that these rules were a bit overboard, a bit too strict, let me say something. My friend, we live in a world governed by self-gratification. Society tells us, "If it feels good, do it" and "It's my life and I'll do what I want." For years I lived by those rules—it was a selfish life of uncontrolled indulgence, and it brought me to ruin.

Paul warns, "Do not be deceived; neither fornicators, nor idolaters, nor adulterers, nor effeminate, nor homosexuals, nor thieves, nor the covetous, nor drunkards, nor revilers, nor swindlers, shall inherit the kingdom of God. And such *were* some of you; but you were washed, but you were sanctified, but you were justified in the name of the Lord Jesus Christ, and in the Spirit of our God" (1 Cor. 6:9-11, emphasis added).

The operative word in this passage is "were"—past tense. My past life with its immorality and deceit, as far as I was concerned, was history.

EXTREME PERSONAL LESSON:

When Jesus Christ comes into your life, the wicked lifestyle goes out. If you call yourself a Christian, then live in a manner worthy of your calling. If you're not going to live a holy life, then change your name to "heathen."

As a new Christian, I was learning how to exercise self-control and to live a life subjected to God and His Holy Spirit. I didn't see it as bondage but as freedom. I was finally free from my screaming carnal man. He was put in his place thanks to the godly guidance of the staff at Twin Oaks Academy. They believed Jeri and I belonged together but were concerned that physical desire would override spiritual growth. They knew that most relationships are based on lust, not love. I already had traveled down that road—been there, done that. As a nonbeliever, whatever I wanted I grabbed. Now the Lord was teaching me patience. I was learning the powerful lesson of seeking *first* the kingdom of God and *His* righteousness.

But finally it was time. Our 15 minutes had come. I met Jeri on the boardwalk, and we strolled along side-by-side, not touching. A few hundred yards from our point of departure was a fence, a barn and a few dozen cows. I couldn't go any farther—time would not permit it. This would have to be "the place"—not exactly dripping with romance but, hey, it would have to do.

I turned, faced Jeri and looked into her beautiful sparkling eyes. The sun glistened in her hair. My words were simple and direct, "Jeri, I love you. Will you marry me?" Her response melted my heart. "Steve, I love you, too. How could I say no? Yes! I'll marry you."

At that very moment a large brown cow, standing nearby and serving as a witness to our big moment, bellowed out a consenting "Mooo." It was magic! In a "normal" marriage proposal, this was the moment when the man would give his newly betrothed an engagement ring. I had nothing—not even a pull-top from a soda can. But it didn't matter.

EXTREME PERSONAL LESSON:

**When a cow consents to your marriage proposal,
you are destined for great marital bliss.
(Just kidding!)**

Jeri and I smiled and held each other's gaze for as long as time allowed. Most newly engaged couples kiss and embrace. Not us. Remember, no PDA. I looked at my watch, our 15 minutes were up. It was time to go, so we parted company and headed back to our dorms. Glancing back I said, "See ya' later, Jeri." She replied, "Talk to you tomorrow, Steve. Bye." Sound strange? Maybe so, but it was a unique beginning to a wonderful, enduring relationship.

Determine in your heart to submit to God and the authorities He has placed over you. Seek His face. Follow His leadership. Commit your ways to the Lord. The psalmist writes, "Delight yourself in the LORD; and He will give you the desires of your heart. Commit your way to the LORD, trust also in Him, and He will do it" (Ps. 37:4-5).

The things you desire and need in life will come your way as you seek first His kingdom and as you dare to be one of those who follows Christ completely.

Welcome to War

CHAPTER FIVE

EXTREME LESSON:

Christianity is not a life of comfort but of conflict. Anyone who chooses to become a Christian automatically enters God's military and is immediately engaged in the longest war ever fought.

"For our struggle is not against flesh and blood, but against the rulers, against the powers, against the world forces of this darkness, against the spiritual forces of wickedness in the heavenly places."

EPHESIANS 6:12

When Jeri and I got engaged, we had no idea what our future held. If you had told me then that I would one day be preaching to millions of people and holding crusades around the world, I would have said you were a false prophet. But if you had told me that Jeri and I would have an incredibly awesome marriage, I would have believed you. She was definitely the right girl for me.

One day David Wilkerson came into the cafeteria at Twin Oaks looking for someone to wash and wax his car. I desperately needed the money and he paid well, so my hand shot up like a rocket. That afternoon, while buffing his automobile, he came over to check out my work. I took the opportunity to tell him that Jeri and I were now engaged. Viewing him as a prophet of God, I knew he could rebuke or bless our plans, and Jeri and I both desired his blessing. His words were music to my ears, "Steve, you've got the best girl on the ranch." Now, after two decades of marriage (we are approaching our silver anniversary), I add a hardy *amen*!

After completing the academic segment at Twin Oaks, Jeri and I decided to spend our engagement period, which turned out to be one year, at Outreach Ministries. Jim Summers had employed several of the female graduates, including Jeri, to start a girls' program. My job description in the ministry ranged from teaching on the men's farm (the men's home was now a girls' home and the men had moved outside the city), publishing the newsletter, evangelizing and whatever else Jim needed.

Our times together were much longer and more frequent now, but we were still under supervision and strict guidelines. Our day off was Monday and that's when we grew to know one another. The wedding was right around the corner, so Jeri and I began mowing lawns and raking leaves in order to pay for it. I had already painted a house to purchase her ring and will never forget how proud I felt when I slipped it on her finger.

We were married at my mom's church, St. Mark's Lutheran Church in Huntsville on April 7, 1979. The place was filled to capacity with about 300 of our family and friends in attendance. It was a very '70s wedding—the best man and groomsmen wore powder-blue suits because we could not afford tuxes. To cover all the bases, we had a Pentecostal and a Lutheran pastor officiate the ceremony. Jeri and I had written our own vows—we were ready.

After the simple yet beautiful ceremony, we set off for our week-long honeymoon in Gatlinburg, Tennessee, in a car given to us as a gift by our dear friends from Twin Oaks. Our wedding was on Saturday, and on Sunday we were in church in Gatlinburg. The pastor welcomed us and then went into shock when he found out we had just gotten married.

I'll never forget his statement to the church, "How many of you went to church on your honeymoon?" It was a gentle rebuke, but what he was really saying was, "Some of you folks cling to any excuse to keep from going to church and here we have a young couple on their honeymoon in the house of God."

This may seem trivial to you, but I'd just like to point out that many believers today don't want to endure any inconveniences or suffering. So many times we avoid whatever might upset our own plans. I've met students about to graduate Bible school who talked more about their desired salary and benefits package than their burden for souls.

After we were married, many of our friends were bringing in healthy salaries and living in stately homes while we were making $60 a week. Don't get me wrong—I'm not complaining. Jeri and I had been miraculously rescued from certain destruction (you'll read her remarkable testimony later in the book) and we were so thankful to be alive. Everything we had belonged to Jesus, and it was a joy to give to Him, even when it was just a few dollars.

This chapter is entitled "Welcome to War" as a reminder that Christians should never forget that much of the battle is fought in the mind. In my early years as a believer, there were plenty of opportunities for Satan to cloud the issue and insert a little of his poison. Questions would arise in my mind like, *How come they're so blessed and we're not?* or *They're eating at that fancy restaurant and all we can afford is the Super Value meal combo.* Be careful! These little pity parties can fester and turn into full-blown attacks. Cut them off at the pass and, like Paul, thank God for whatever state you are in. "Not that I speak from want; for I have learned to be content in whatever circumstances I am" (Phil. 4:11).

Allow the seed of God's Word to fall on the fertile soil of your heart. "Let your character be free from the love of money, being content with what you have; for He Himself has said, 'I will never desert you, nor will I ever forsake you'" (Heb. 13:5).

EXTREME PERSONAL LESSON:

A complaining spirit will cut you off from God's blessings. Learn to take authority over any thoughts that would drive a wedge between you and Jesus.

To this day I believe God saw our faithfulness in the little things and in turn entrusted us with much more. After all, why would God bless you with thousands if He can't trust you with hundreds? If He can't trust you to tithe on $10, why should He give you $100?

Let me tell you about our first humble digs. We lived in Huntsville in a factory mill house built in the early 1900s. There was no indoor bathroom until I built one. Roaches and rats ran free—they had lived there for generations and dined on treats from Terminex like it was candy.

At night, after a long church service, Jeri and I would come home and begin our standard evening routine. She would wait patiently on the front porch while I entered the house. With a flick of the light switch, I'd let out a blood-curdling war cry. Hoards of roaches and creatures of the night would flee in all directions. I would then do something akin to an Indian war dance, wildly stomping my feet, until I was sure they had all scattered. Only then would Jeri receive the "coast is clear" call.

Regardless of our tactical maneuvers, the war with these creepy crawlies was never won. One night I loaded a BB gun, camped out in the corner of the living room and waited. The battle lines had been drawn. I was taking the offense position. It was kill or be killed. But there was one problem—it was dark. I could hear them but couldn't see to shoot. Oh, how I could've used some night-vision binoculars to change the destiny of these four-legged demons!

Our home was a hodgepodge of odds and ends. On garbage days I made it a habit to drive the ministry pickup truck to the rich section of town. You'd be surprised what some people throw out. After a couple of hours, my truck bed would be filled to capacity. A quick inventory would reveal a good 8x10-foot roll of lime-green shag carpet, an orange couch with one leg missing, a kitchen chair that needed a little glue and, of course, miscellaneous cans of paint. (No matter what color paint I brought home, after mixing it together it always turned out some shade of green.)

The master bedroom was our pride and joy simply because it contained two brand new items: a mattress we had bought on credit for $10 a month and a $24.99 piece of sky-blue carpet bought with cash. What a suite!

Early on in our marriage I received a call from the steering committee of a large church. Over the phone the deacon made me an enticing offer: "Steve, our church is in desperate need of an associate pastor, and we believe you're the man for the job. We'll offer you $32,000 a year, a car paid for by the church plus a healthy housing allowance. Will you come?"

The carrot was dangling in front of me. All I had to do was grab it, but I already knew the answer: "Fuhgeddaboutit!" God had Jeri and me right where He wanted us. "I'm sorry," I said, "We're not interested. Thanks so much for the offer." I hung up the phone realizing Jesus had total control of my life. He was my Master, not money.

"No one can serve two masters. Either he will hate the one and love the other, or he will be devoted to the one and despise the other. You cannot serve both God and Money" (Matt. 6:24, *NIV*).

I wonder how many pastors and evangelists are motivated by money? I wonder how many have sold their God-given call for a few extra dollars? I tremble at the thought.

Of course, there's nothing wrong with a good salary, a fancy car and a nice home. But to pursue the ministry for the benefits is like building a house on sand. The storms will come and the house will fall.

EXTREME PERSONAL LESSON:

Carefully examine your motives. The will of God is not determined by personal prosperity but by obedience to His perfect plan.

From the very beginning, Jeri and I loved ministry. We sought out ways to lead people to Jesus. On Saturdays, you'd find us roaming our neighborhood and cramming kids into our pickup truck to bring to our backyard for a fun time of Bible lessons, songs and refreshments. We were extremely aggressive with our faith, but not everyone approved of our fervor.

Despite our contentment at being in the center of God's will, this was also a time of intense spiritual warfare. It wasn't uncommon for me to spend hours on end reasoning with and praying over a young drug addict. The chains of hell would break loose and snap when hit by the power of Jesus Christ. Hell had him bound; heaven would set him free. It was spiritual warfare and the stakes were high—his soul was the spoil of war.

Life also offered some strange twists and turns. Late one night, someone came banging on our front door. I answered and found a rough-looking man staring me in the face. "You the preacher who's been talkin' to my boy in your backyard about God?" he bellowed.

He sure didn't look happy. Was he there to belt me or bless me? I stared him down and said, "Yes, sir, that's me. My name is Steve. What can I do for you?"

His reply caught me by surprise. "Well, I just came by to say thanks. Bobby quit stealing from stores, and he's been a better kid around the house. He even obeys me now. Whatever you're doing, preacher, keep it up!" With that, he stomped off into the night.

To help with finances, Jeri and I talked about her getting a secular job. She was more than happy to and wound up working at the local library. Her assignment was to send out books requested by the blind and the handicapped. The library had a wide selection of all types of literature. But when someone asked for a particular book full of sex and violence, Jeri would suggest something more wholesome. Since becoming a Christian, her high standards and convictions were set in stone.

This soon came to the attention of her boss who called her into his office one day to request she justify her actions. Careful not to condemn, Jeri explained how, as a Christian, she could not be a part of polluting the minds of others. Her response was accepted, and she was allowed to stay at her job. Someone else was put in charge of sending out the more questionable literature.

Jeri had fulfilled Scripture by being an example of holiness. "Let no one look down on your youthfulness, but rather in speech, conduct, love, faith and purity, show yourself an example of those who believe" (1 Tim. 4:12).

Jeri started an early morning Bible study and prayer time at the library. It was well attended and became the highlight of the day for many employees. Several were saved through these efforts, and Jesus was glorified.

EXTREME PERSONAL LESSON:

Use every opportunity as a mission field. Grab a plow, bag up some seed, put a sickle over your shoulder and get to work.

In 1981, after several years with Outreach Ministries, God called us to move on. I took a position as youth pastor at an Assemblies of God church in Panama City, Florida. While at this church, God tested me in a way that had never occurred before.

During one of our morning services, a young mother with a baby in her arms and two toddlers in tow came forward for prayer. To her right and left was a prayer line of at least two dozen people wanting prayer. The procedure was simple, and I had done it hundreds of times before. We pastors would lay hands on each person, pray God would meet their needs and then proceed with the service. These were powerful times, and we often witnessed the miracle-working hand of God.

When I came to this young mother, the Lord stopped me and said, "Ask her what she needs." She explained how her husband had left and she was now responsible for two small children and her baby. Her home was several miles from the church, and they had no mode of transportation. She needed a car.

I had seen God provide before, so I laid hands on her forehead and began to cry out to Jesus for His provision. Then, out of the blue, came these words, "Your car is her car."

I must be hearing things, I thought. *What was that?*

"Your car is her car." I knew this couldn't be God simply because Jeri and I had only one car. Our only other mode of transportation were two 10-speed Huffys from Wal-Mart. Surely it was a mistake. Then it happened again, "Your car is her car."

I started a serious, silent discussion with the Lord while still praying aloud for the woman. Silently I pleaded my case to the Lord. "Jesus, we have only one car. Our Pontiac Sunbird is paid for in full and runs great. There are people in this congregation who have two and three cars. Let me make an announcement and see what floats to the surface."

"Your car is her car," again came the reply.

Determined not to let my Sunbird fly away, I began to negotiate. "Jesus, tell You what we'll do. The church has several vans. We'll faithfully pick her up for every service and take her back home."

"Your car is her car."

"Jesus, Jeri and I would be more than happy to loan her our car whenever she needs it."

"Your car is her car."

I was fighting a losing battle. In a last-ditch effort, I called my wife over. "Jeri," I said, "the Lord is speaking to me about giving this lady our car." I was certain my faithful, Pontiac Sunbird-loving wife would set God straight. I was wrong. She sided with the Lord and said, "Then you better do it!"

The battle was over. The next day the lady came by the church, we signed the papers, and she drove away in the answer to her prayer request.

God taught me a powerful lesson. Everything I have is His; I am only a steward of His property. If He chooses to redistribute some of His possessions, who am I to object?

The story doesn't end there. This took place in the summer of 1981. Seventeen years later, in 1998, I was handed a note while seated on the platform at the Brownsville Revival in Pensacola, Florida. I had been preaching for three years at this Holy Ghost outpouring. Millions had come from all over the world to receive a miracle touch from God.

I unfolded the small handwritten letter. It read,

My name is Melissa. Many years ago in Panama City I came to your church seeking help. I was going through a very difficult time in my life and desperately needed a miracle. My greatest need was finding transportation, and you supplied that need by giving me your only car. I am sending this note, through a friend, to say thanks. I now live in Maine. The car wore out several years ago, but the spiritual benefits of what you did will remain forever. Because of your obedience my three children and I were able to attend church for many years. Thanks to you, they're all serving God today. You made their spiritual growth possible by your sacrificial gift. Thank you, and God bless you!

EXTREME PERSONAL LESSON:

It's easy to give out of our surplus but much more difficult to give sacrificially. Everything we have belongs to God—hold nothing back.

Although I had been in the ministry for several years, I was constantly being tested for my faithfulness. It was as if God was checking me out. Leonard Ravenhill used to tell me that obedience was the most important characteristic of the Christian life. He would say that God is looking for a few people He can trust. He is still looking for those who are willing to learn the lessons and dare to obey Him completely.

**WANTED:
EXTREME
CHRISTIANS**

You Are Not Your Own

CHAPTER SIX

EXTREME LESSON:

The true follower of Jesus Christ lives with the understanding that God is now the One who dictates direction.

"Or do you not know that your body is a temple of the Holy Spirit who is in you, whom you have from God, and that you are not your own? For you have been bought with a price: therefore glorify God in your body."

I CORINTHIANS 6:19-20

You just read five of the most life-changing words in the Holy Bible: *You are not your own.* These words have served as a catalyst to launch thousands of men and women into world missions. They've been *morning reveille* to the backslidden believer, a clarion call to the calloused Christian. The revelation of who we are and who He is can send spiritual shock waves through the lives of slacker saints, causing them to erupt with a righteous zeal that has set nations on fire and sparked revival. I'm talking to you about the call of God—the heart-wrenching, life-altering, career-changing, all-demanding call of God.

I gotta tell you—as I write this, my hands are actually trembling. I believe it's because of a deep reverential fear that causes me to shudder when discussing with anyone the call of God. The reason for my fear will become obvious as you read on.

Don't be offended by the words that follow. They are written with great care and a holy sensitivity to the reader, but at the same time they must separate the complacent Sunday-morning socialite from the serious, blood-washed saint.

You see, there exists a crisis in today's Church that if not dealt with, will carry consequences of catastrophic proportions. Hell holds captive the fallout from the damage that's already been done. We must confront this issue.

I'm talking about the clergy, those in ministry. I'm talking about those who wear the cloak but don't carry the call; those who love self more than souls, their own words more than His Word and the life of the ministry more than the Lord of the ministry. There are many who actively take part in leading other soldiers, while they themselves have never completed boot camp. They bellow out orders to those below them but can't hear the mandates from the King above. They're trying to lead others into the deeper things of God yet are completely oblivious to the shallowness of their own souls. They can prepare a sermon using the latest in Bible software and grip their audience with the polished eloquence of a trendy motivational speaker, but they are at a loss for words when it comes to delivering a sinner from the grips of hell.

You may be saying to yourself, *Steve, you're going overboard. Why be so harsh? Surely this is just an overreaction to a few negative encounters you've experienced over the years.*

Friend, I say this because the eternal destiny of countless souls is in the balance. Do you realize we have young men in the ministry today, not because they're called, but simply because they're following in their father's footsteps? As if this were some kind of secular business, they slip on their corporate robes, grab a Bible and head out into the church world. They have the approval of their earthly dad, but they have failed to check with their heavenly Father. Their heads are full of dazzling ideas, but their hearts are void of divine inspiration.

The opposite situation is almost equally as dangerous. Did you know it's entirely possible to be swept into the river of revival, be set ablaze by the fire of the Holy Ghost, sense a spiritual sensation when souls are being saved, feel the ecstasy of heavenly worship and still not be called to the ministry? Did you know that someone can deeply love God, even be in preparation for full-time ministry, and still be missing God's call?

EXTREME PERSONAL LESSON:

An intense, all-consuming love for Holy Ghost revival is not a divine indicator that you are called into the ministry.

Today's Church is full of self-proclaimed prophets, pastors, apostles, teachers and evangelists. The five-fold ministry of the

Church has become the five flavors of fortune. Some are like a modern-day Demas, who fall into a pit of prosperity and choose to never climb out. "For Demas, having loved this present world, has deserted me" (2 Tim. 4:10). They started out with a legitimate calling but ended up falling.

Other men and women of the cloth are able to hide their deceptive plots behind ministerial masks, but eventually they are exposed. We hear about their sexual sins or financial fiascos as they unfold in the media. They often escape punishment with just a slap on the wrist, while true men and women of the cloth are left heartbroken, ashamed that once again their sacred calling has been smeared by counterfeit clergy.

Nothing much can be done about the wolves disguised as sheep who are slipping into the flock. Matthew 7:15 tells us, "Beware of the false prophets, who come to you in sheep's clothing, but inwardly are ravenous wolves." These deceivers will always be among us. Second Timothy 3:13 (*KJV*) says, "But evil men and seducers shall wax worse and worse, deceiving, and being deceived." Apart from ripping off their sheep's clothing to expose their true identity, the best thing we can do is to place them in the hands of a vengeful God.

There's something else we can do. I suggest we focus on getting holy, God-called, Jesus-loving men and women into mainstream ministry.

I recently read of the board of a major U.S. corporation that decided to demote its CEO and promote another, after the stark realization that they had the wrong man for the job. They had a private trying to be a general. The stock was plummeting, the shareholders were furious, and change was desperately needed. For the corporation it was a do-or-die situation.

The same is true in the recruitment and placement of ministers of the Gospel. Some men and women in church leadership have no idea how to manage God's business. They need to bow out, get before the Lord and identify their true purpose in life.

My point is that it's wrong to place ourselves in full-time ministry when Jesus has a totally different plan and purpose for our lives.

Here's how I identify a call to ministry—it's what I refer to as the Five Proofs of a Call to the Ministry. These have been gleaned from my 25 years of ministry—25 years of studying the great works of men and women of God and 25 years of watching the Body of Christ suffer from overexposure to ministers who are suffering from underexposure to Christ.

In this chapter, these five proofs serve as your Extreme Personal Lessons. Read over them. Pray over them. Examine your life in the light of God's Word. As Peter writes, this is to help you make your election and calling sure. "Therefore, brethren, be all the more diligent to make certain about His calling and choosing you; for as long as you practice these things, you will never stumble" (2 Pet. 1:10).

Do you feel the weight of the mantle of ministry? Has God's burden for the lost become your burden? The Lord of the harvest is looking for loyal laborers. Perhaps God has given you a divine mandate.

I emphasize to you the seriousness of such a call. This is not a pretend war game with plastic bullets and a make-believe enemy. This is real! In fact, this is the longest, toughest war ever fought.

My goal in this chapter is to lay a foundation for identifying God's call. I'll help you answer questions like, *Where am I now and where does God want to take me? How can I be certain Jesus wants me to enter full-time ministry? Is it possible to be assured of my assignment?*

If God uses the ideas in this chapter to sift out even just a few of the called from the uncalled, my efforts will have been worthwhile.

Let's start by setting the record straight. Everyone is called to be part of God's kingdom. Peter says, "The Lord is not slow about His promise, as some count slowness, but is patient toward you, not wishing for any to perish but for all to come to repentance" (2 Pet. 3:9).

Every single one of us should be actively sharing the love of Jesus with those around us.

PROOF 1:

A person called to the ministry will definitely have a deep, genuine love for the Savior.

Maybe this one sounds like a no-brainer, but please hear me out. This is a major road sign on the ministry highway. After all, doesn't the book of Matthew tell us that loving God is the first and foremost commandment? "'You shall love the LORD your God with all your heart, and with all your soul, and with all your mind.' This is the great and foremost commandment" (Matt. 22:37-38).

It's a sad truth that there are thousands of men and women working in full-time ministry today who lack a true love and commitment to Jesus Christ, the Head of the Church. Why do you think the following words are found in the Sermon on the Mount?

> Not every one who says to Me, "Lord, Lord," will enter the kingdom of heaven; but he who does the will of My Father who is in heaven. Many will say to me on that day, "Lord, Lord, did we not prophesy in Your name, and in Your name cast out demons, and in Your name perform many miracles?" And then I will declare to them, "I never

knew you; depart from Me, you who practice lawless-
ness" (Matt. 7:21-23).

In my Bible, these words are in red—direct from our Lord's
lips. Jesus didn't say that they tried to cast out devils; He said
that they did! Jesus didn't say that they tried to prophesy; He
said that they did! Jesus didn't say that they attempted to do
many wonderful works; He said that they did! All this was done
under the banner of Christianity.

The problem was not their labor in the ministry but rather
their love for the Messiah. They did everything outside the
Lordship of Jesus Christ. My friend, before you begin preaching
about the love of God, you must experience the love of God—up
close and personal. God would never call someone into His
work without his or her first having developed a deep love for
His Son.

Other words of Jesus that should be ringing in our ears were
spoken directly to one of His disciples. Jesus peppered Peter with
this question, "Peter, do you love Me? Peter, do you love Me?
Peter, do you love Me?" (see John 21:15-17). We know Peter's
response. If you don't, study your Bible.

Do you love Jesus? Have you been saved from sin and filled
with His Holy Spirit? As the old hymn "Are You Washed in the
Blood" asks, "Have you been to Jesus for the cleansing power, are
you washed in the blood of the Lamb?"

God won't place someone in such a strategic position as a
minister of His Gospel without first seeing "salvation" on his or
her spiritual resumé. You've got to go to the Cross before carrying credentials. You must have already traded the love of mam-
mon for the love of the Messiah.

If you're not in love with Jesus, you have no business in
the ministry. Before you enter His fields, make sure you live
in His favor.

PROOF 2:

A person who is called to the ministry will sense a deep recognition that they are not their own but were bought with a price.

I've already shared this verse, but it bears repeating, "Do you not know that your body is a temple of the Holy Spirit who is in you, whom you have from God, and that you are not your own? For you have been bought with a price: therefore glorify God in your body" (1 Cor. 6:19-20).

A true Christian no longer calls the shots. Christ is not only a Savior, but He is also Lord of everything. Stamped on that person is a sign that reads "God's property. Paid for in full."

The truth is, as believers, we are not our own to waste time in idleness. We are not our own to follow after worldly desires and affections. We are not our own to serve self. As Charles Spurgeon once said, "Self is a dethroned tyrant." We are now part of the family of God—the old is gone, the new has come. It's time to glorify Jesus Christ with our lives.

There's one statement you may have heard me make repeatedly. I've spoken it into the mind and heart of a tender seven-year-old boy and turned right around and whispered it into the ear of a 70-year-old grandma.

They are simple yet powerful words: Jesus loves you, and He has a wonderful plan for your life. Some folks burst into tears as these words are spoken. Others force a smile, saying, "But how can I know His plan?" My response? Draw close to Jesus. Read His Word. Stay in an on-fire, Bible-preaching church and remember you are not your own; you belong to Jesus. Let Him have His way in your life.

The proof of this ownership plays out in decisions we make throughout our Christian lives. Let me give you a personal example.

In 1984, while on a missions trip to Mexico, a missionary talked to us about the need for church planters in Argentina and encouraged us to pray about going there. Soon after this conversation, the Lord opened the door for Jeri and me to spend a month ministering in this land of the gauchos. That's all it took. We were hooked.

From that moment on, we had our hearts set and our sails hoisted toward Buenos Aires. We knew that Argentina was going to be our new home. We would eat, drink and sleep Argentina, but, oh, how we were tested.

Let me ask you this: Have you ever had your heart set on something and then things didn't turn out the way you wanted? Maybe you had your eyes on a certain automobile, maybe a fire-engine-red Mustang convertible. You saw it one day, in all its glory, at the local dealership. They had just hosed it off. It glistened. A little voice spoke clearly, "Behold, your next car!"

As you approached the vehicle, the salesman approached his victim—you. His words were almost prophetic and confirmed your deepest feelings. "My friend, are you looking for some good, reliable transportation?"

Wow! How did he know I was looking for a car? Hooked, but not yet in the boat, the salesman starts reeling in his catch. "This dream machine is a one-owner, low-mileage, fully-loaded, below-book-value bargain. The previous owner, a dear sister at the local Catholic church, decided to trade it in for something more conservative. Just about every mile on the odometer is a Mass mile. That's right, just back and forth to church. I've never seen a car in better condition."

That's all it took—you were hooked. You just had to have that car. The next few days were jammed with fervent prayer.

You dreamed about it, you talked about it, you even carried around a picture of it. You named it and claimed it. You even shifted into spiritual overdrive by slipping down to the car lot after closing and marching around your miracle, sounding a triumphant shofar. It wasn't yet parked at your home, but it was definitely parked in your heart.

Then one bright sunny day, with down payment in hand, you arrived at the dealership only to find your miracle was now a mirage. Someone else had slipped in and purchased your promise. Your heart sank. It took weeks to repair your shipwrecked soul.

All this may sound silly, but it happens every day. People lose a car, get turned down for a job, are denied a loan for a house, receive a letter of rejection from a university—the list goes on and on. Disappointments are a part of life.

Jeri and I had our hearts tuned to the Argentine frequency. It was *our* fire-engine-red Mustang convertible. As part of missionary induction with the Assemblies of God, every new couple must sit before the executive board of its Division of Foreign Missions for a time of evaluation. It was our turn. We gathered around a massive, beautiful wooden table with gray-haired, seasoned servants of the Lord who represented the four corners of the globe.

Their combined wisdom could fill volumes on how to fulfill the Great Commission. They had slashed through jungles and ridden camels through blistering deserts. They had scaled mountains in search of lost tribes, planted churches and started Bible schools.

These men were now in charge of our lives. The executive director, J. Philip Hogan, welcomed us and asked, "We understand you want to work in Argentina. Is that correct?"

"Yes sir," I said. "Argentina is in desperate need of church planters, and we feel God could use us there." I felt as if my case had been stated decisively. We were standing firm on our call.

"That's all fine and good," he said, "but what if we wanted

you to go to Africa? We need missionaries to forge new territory among the African people. How about it?"

Now, you must understand the intensity of the moment. Our future was on the line. Our hearts were set on Argentina, and in our eyes the only thing the jungles of Africa had in common with Argentina was that they're on the same planet.

I glanced at Jeri, and she smiled. Looking Brother Hogan straight in the eyes, I said, "Fine, whatever you brothers want us to do. Whatever you feel is God's plan for our lives is OK with us. We just want to serve the Lord."

Dead silence filled the room. Our answer apparently had come as a shock. These men were accustomed to hearing young bucks like myself raise their voice in a rebellious response, "God has called us to Argentina, and that's where we're going—*period!*" But they heard the opposite from us. Why? Because Jeri and I did not own our lives. We were servants of the Most High and sitting before us were His chosen leaders.

With a contented look, Brother Hogan slowly grinned and said, "Aw, you can go to Argentina."

Whew! It was a test to see if we were going to respond as rebellious rookies or submit as surrendered servants. We passed. Those truly called to the ministry live with a deep recognition that they are not their own.

The next three proofs are almost self-explanatory. Although we won't spend as much time discussing them, they are still part of the basic foundation of the call of God.

PROOF 3:

A person called into the ministry has a constant desire to be useful to God.

A person called into the ministry will possess a burning desire to be at His service. Young or old, one who is truly called will be preoccupied with the work of the Lord and will do anything to please God. No job is too menial, no task too difficult. Everything is done for Jesus.

Paul put it this way, "And whatever you do in word or deed, do all in the name of the Lord Jesus, giving thanks through Him to God the Father" (Col. 3:17).

The cry of the Great Commission is like a trumpet blast from heaven. Those who are called want to do what Jesus wants them to do:

> Go therefore and make disciples of all the nations, baptizing them in the name of the Father and the Son and the Holy Spirit, teaching them to observe all that I commanded you; and lo, I am with you always, even to the end of the age (Matt. 28:19-20).

Do you find yourself always wanting to help out at church? Are you excited about being involved in church regardless of the task? Are you one of the 20 percent who do the majority of the work around the house of God, while the remaining 80 percent pursue other interests? When the pastor asks for a volunteer, does your hand shoot up?

Friend, these are all signs that you enjoy being useful to God. Of course, there are dear Christians in the Church who love the work of the Lord but are not called to full-time ministry. However, you cannot be in full-time ministry if there does not exist a desire to do something for God.

Do you feel the urgency of the hour? Do you want to do something beneficial in the Kingdom before it's too late? "We must work the works of Him who sent Me, as long as it is day; night is coming, when no man can work" (John 9:4). Does this

Bible verse compel you to make a difference? If so, perhaps God has laid upon you the mantle of full-time ministry.

The other day, a young man was asking me questions, searching for a confirmation of his call to the ministry. I questioned his sincerity and commitment—it seemed he wanted to jump right into holding large crusades without paying any kind of price.

He was humbled when I challenged him by saying, "Do you really want to be used of God? Then get a Bible, a box and go out into a city park. Climb up on your little platform and begin preaching. Get busy for God. Do something for Him."

PROOF 4:

A person called into the ministry will have a deep love and compassion for souls.

My computer screensaver contains one large word. It moves from right to left, left to right and up and down. It's the word "souls."

Love for souls brought Jesus down from heaven. Love for souls will send you out into the world. Jesus showed compassion on the lost, and we are to do the same.

In the first chapter of this book, I talked about a young man who screamed out during one of our crusades. My response was not condemnation but compassion. A true disciple of Jesus Christ is known by the love he has for his fellow man.

During all our crusades, we open up the altars for special prayer. In some countries, we are literally crushed by the crowds of people pressing in for a touch from God. I have had my hands grabbed and found myself jerked over the heads of the people. Hungry souls are screaming out, "Touch me! Touch me!"

A true minister of the Gospel will spend his life serving fresh bread and water to the starving masses. He will care for the fatherless and champion the cause of the widows. The drug addict dying of AIDS, the skid-row drunk reeking of alcohol, the little child in tattered clothing, the mom on welfare who can give only a widow's mite, the teen who comes dressed in leather and chains, the businessman with a big bank account but an empty heart, the gray-haired grandma who's too feeble to walk—these are all children of God who've been entrusted to the care of His ministers.

If you don't love them—all of them—stay out of the ministry. Luke describes how Jesus hung out with sinners, "Now all the tax-gatherers and the sinners were coming near Him to listen to Him. And both the Pharisees and the scribes began to grumble, saying, 'This man receives sinners and eats with them'" (Luke 15:1-2). Christ was persecuted by the pious snobs for dining with derelicts. Oh, how He loved them.

The apostle Paul, when speaking of such love, took the challenge outside the four walls of the church by saying, "And may the Lord cause you to increase and abound in love for one another, and for all men, just as we also do for you" (1 Thess. 3:12).

PROOF 5:

Any other type of vocation or employment seems uninviting to those called into the ministry.

This is not to say that secular employment is unimportant or unnecessary; rather, it becomes secondary to the call of God. We all know that Paul labored with his hands to supplement his ministry income. When we read the following verse, it's important to understand that money was not Paul's goal; rather, it was to further the kingdom of God. "Nor did we eat anyone's bread without paying for it, but with labor and hardship we kept working night and day so that we might not be a burden to any of you" (2 Thess. 3:8).

A man or woman of God who is truly called would rather work for Jesus in some God-forsaken corner of the world than live in the lap of luxury. A young man once approached me with tears in his eyes. He was in a dilemma. His father, a successful businessman, had offered him a six-figure salary, a new car and a home if he would join the family business. The young man turned him down. Now, after one year of Bible school, the father was once again pressuring him.

The son's comments to me illustrate well these five proofs of a call to ministry. He explained, "Steve, several years ago I gave my life to Jesus, and I have been in love with Him ever since. Only being about my heavenly Father's business makes me happy. When I see lost souls, I feel their pain. I don't want anyone to go to hell. All I want to do is work in the vineyard of the Lord. I love my family and respect my dad's offer, but I've got to do what the Lord has called me to do."

Friend, that's a young man obviously called to the ministry.

Take these proofs and lay them before the Lord. Don't be afraid. Remember, "For the gifts and the calling of God are irrevocable" (Rom. 11:29). If you're called, come! Enter the work of the Lord without reservation. No strings attached. Be one of those who dare to obey Christ completely.

Captured Alive

CHAPTER SEVEN

EXTREME LESSON:

Jesus left this earth after issuing a mandate to His followers. He didn't say to pray about going; He said to just do it.

"Go therefore and make disciples of all the nations, baptizing them in the name of the Father and the Son and the Holy Spirit, teaching them to observe all that I have commanded you; and lo, I am with you always, even to the end of the age."

MATTHEW 28:19-20

How do I describe the emotion of the day? There we were, on the streets of Mexico City, with 10 teenagers from our church in Tallahassee, Florida. It was 1984, and Jeri and I were in our third year as youth pastors at Evangel Assembly of God. We had decided to take some of the more serious youth on a mission trip to Mexico. This would be my first time out of the country as a Christian. I had crossed the border years earlier through the town of Nogales, New Mexico, but that was in search of cheaper pot and tequila parties. Now I was entering to share the love of Jesus.

We were surrounded by the sights, sounds and smells of another culture. Mexico City, the fast-paced, second most-populated metropolis in the world, took me by surprise. Every time we boarded a bus, I thought for sure we were breaking the world record for occupancy. Back in the States we had once celebrated our efforts at cramming a dozen people into a VW Beetle. Here such a feat was an everyday occurrence.

The air had a peculiar smell. It carried the smoke from street sausage vendors and diesel fumes from hundreds of buses. At times I felt as if I were looking through smoked glass. Thousands of uninspected cars and taxis raced by, spewing exhaust into the air. A kind English-speaking businessman explained to me that breathing one day on the city streets of Mexico was the same as smoking a whole pack of cigarettes. I believed him.

Fresh fruit was on sale right next to bins of fried grasshoppers. Fly-covered meat was dangling from hooks in open-air markets. Peddlers were everywhere, calling out the bargain of the day. Shoeshine men insisted that our *zapatos* were dull and lifeless and for only a quarter we could be walking in style.

We were captured alive by the needs of the people there. Beggars sat perched like birds on steps, street corners and flattened cardboard boxes. They never failed to reach out a hand to the rich North Americans passing by. We stuck out like black-birds in snow. "Un peso, por favor. Necesito algo para comer. Ayudame." (Please give me a peso. I need something to eat. Help me.) We tossed a few coins into the cup.

I knew my donation was more for me than the beggar. It was a way of pacifying a gnawing feeling inside me that something was wrong. Why was there such a chasm between the "haves" and the "have-nots"? What we Americans stuff down our garbage disposals could easily feed multitudes of Mexico's starving.

That evening, after a wonderful service in a small local church, the Lord began speaking to me: *Steve, you will always have the poor. Don't ever forget that their spiritual poverty far exceeds their physical poverty. I am calling you. You can make a difference.*

The next morning I awoke with a new perspective. What good was it to give them a temporal meal down here if I didn't invite them to the eternal banquet up there? A loaf of bread lasts a few moments or days, but the Bread of Life lasts forever. I could try to clothe, feed and house the downtrodden, but if I didn't lead them to Jesus, they were no better off than before. So we decided to get busy.

Jeri and I spent most of that day standing on a smog-filled street corner holding an open box of tracts. With tears streaming down our faces, we watched hundreds of people grab the tiny pieces of literature and begin reading, consuming them as if they were bits of food. "Gracias, señor," said one man. "Uno para mi hijo, por favor," said another. (One for my son, please.)

Along came a young mother with a baby strapped to her back, two dirty-faced tots clinging to her arms and a dog following close behind. "Señor. No tenemos leche en la casa. Mi marido se fue. Ayudanos por favor." (We don't have any milk at home. My husband has left. Help us please.) I gave her a dollar and a tract.

At times, we actually had lines form in order to receive a booklet. I watched as some devoured the contents, bowed their heads and prayed the simple prayer found on the last page. That day, our lives were about to take a major turn. Like the believers spoken of in 1 Corinthians 16:15, we were now addicted to the ministry of souls. We knew then that we would one day be living and working south of the border.

Most of our evangelism was done in the early morning or late afternoon. The rest of the day, we worked at the new church site pushing wheelbarrows and toting cement. The work was hard and the sun was hot. I was waiting for the teens to complain, but none of them did.

Their experience in Mexico was not what they had planned. They had their hearts set on evangelizing from sunup to sundown and had practiced drama skits and learned Spanish songs. They were told that every day we would hold street meetings; instead, they were involved in hard, manual labor, because of some miscommunication between the resident missionary and myself. But the situation turned out to be an attitude check from heaven, and all our teens passed with flying colors.

EXTREME PERSONAL LESSON:

When things don't go your way, don't complain. Find a task to do and do it with all your might as unto the Lord.

While in Mexico City, Jeri and I got a chance to talk with Don and Melba Exley, church planters in Argentina, along with their two children. They were taking a year off to plant a church in Mexico and asked us to do something that forever altered the course of our lives.

We were all on a tour bus to the Mexican pyramids when Don said, "Before making up your mind concerning your next missions assignment, please consider Argentina. There is a great revival going on there, and we desperately need church planters." That moment, a seed was dropped into the soil of my heart—a seed that was destined to grow. Nothing would deter us from our challenge to be missionaries for the Lord. The day we returned from Mexico, I resigned my position at the church. Jeri and I had no idea where to go or what to do next, but we knew Jesus would lead us.

We immediately applied with the Assemblies of God (AG) for missionary appointment. Our first conversations with the leadership were like buckets of water on a fiery blaze. They did everything they could to discourage us, and we understood why. Many missionary candidates can be talked out of their calling in a 10-minute phone conversation. They're told of the rough road ahead, the mountain of funds they'll need to raise, the years of preparation and the stress and strain of living on foreign soil. (If you're considering missionary work, remember that it takes about 50 percent of your energy just to survive on foreign soil.) However, the more the AG leadership shared with us, the more excited we got.

Jeri and I had been living a comfortable life. We had stepped up from the mill house in Huntsville and the mobile home in Panama City to a nice three-bedroom, two-bath rental home in Tallahassee. We had just purchased new furniture and were even planning to build our dream home. But life as we knew it was about to change.

Within a few short weeks, we found ourselves on our front lawn standing next to a sign that read "Everything must go!" As Jeri handed out free cookies and iced tea, neighbors, friends and passersby pulled up in trucks to haul off their bargains. When the dust settled, only a few personal items remained.

We then moved into a small apartment and began the painstaking process of raising funds. The apartment was furnished by church folks. Nothing matched. The mattress was stained and the couch was old, but it didn't matter. We were on our way to the fields beyond and were just passing through. We were now full-fledged, full-time missionaries.

My first mistake in preparing for our new life on the road was to buy a small motor home. My banker had warned me it was foolish to shell out money for a gas-guzzling box on wheels, but I didn't listen. I envisioned Jeri and me parked at a roadside campground, somewhere out West, on the itinerate trail. Sitting outside our camper in the cool of the night, we would be counting out thousands of dollars from the offerings that had been pouring in. That dream turned out to be a nightmare.

After doing the math, we realized the bottom line. With just the money we had spent on gas, we could have been staying at expensive hotels. My banker was right; I called him from the frozen tundra of North Dakota. He sympathized with me, realized that this green missionary cadet had learned his lesson and helped us trade it in for a car.

EXTREME PERSONAL LESSON:

When advice is given to you from someone more knowledgeable than you, *listen!* A listening ear can save you from passing through untold heartaches.

Raising funds for missionary support was totally new territory for us. In Tallahassee, I had produced evangelistic Christian festivals that meant raising tens of thousands of dollars through private businesses and individuals. These harvest festivals were geared toward winning the lost, so my approach was always "Help us to help others."

My strategy now was the same, but the figures were much higher. We needed thousands of dollars in monthly support and tens of thousands before we would receive permission to leave for language school in Costa Rica. We were young and excited, and we were blown away by the difficulty of raising missionary support. Getting funds for missions was like going after a piece of pie. Every church had a missions pie with hundreds of missionaries constantly calling and vying for a sliver.

Jeri and I began booking services. We went anywhere and everywhere. We preached in churches that had 10 members in the congregation. We preached in primitive churches in the country and palatial cathedrals in the city. We poured out our hearts, wept over the lost, prayed for the sick and cried out for the people of Argentina. Within eight months, we were approved for departure and found ourselves on an airliner headed for San Jose, Costa Rica.

Jeri and I found a small, furnished house close to the school. We chuckled at an antique washing machine until we realized it was not part of the décor but was actually for washing clothes. We settled in and began the monumental task of language acquisition. Learning another language is like learning to walk— you crawl, you stand, you fall; you crawl, you stand, you fall; you crawl, you stand, you walk, you fall. At times you feel like an absolute idiot. That's good, because you feel like you sound, and the words coming out of your mouth are absolute gibberish.

Many days, we were reduced to tears. Out of sheer frustration, we decided to begin a new program that was geared toward people having difficulty learning the language in a classroom setting. The method was simple, but the learning process was grueling.

We had to memorize several key lines in Spanish. Mine were "My name is Steve Hill. I'm in Costa Rica to learn Spanish. I need to practice what I learn. Would it be possible to live with you?" This was translated into Spanish and recorded onto a small audiocassette for me to memorize. "Mi nombre es Esteban Hill. Estoy en Costa Rica para aprender español. Necesito practicar lo que aprendo. Seria possible vivir contigo?"

Once the student was fluent in these lines, he or she boarded a city bus and went from passenger to passenger until someone offered his or her home. Sound extreme? Sound radical? Sound exciting?

The next step was to move in with that family and become immersed in the culture. On our very first bus ride, three families invited Jeri and me home. We eventually chose a family that had more than one room, moved in and began learning at an unprecedented rate.

You may be thinking, *Steve, I could never do that. My personality could not adapt to such a diverse culture.*

EXTREME PERSONAL LESSON:

With the Lord on your side, you can do all things. He will strengthen you. He will equip you. He will help you, but you must first step out of the boat.

Each day, we memorized and practiced new lines at home and on the streets. Within five months, I was preaching my first message in Spanish. It was short, it was full of mistakes, and it was seasoned with a North American accent, but it was Spanish—and people got saved!

I preached my message in the center of a town called Desamparados on a hot Saturday afternoon. The temperature in Central America doesn't change much during the year—it's always muggy. We had set up a stage and invited a band to play a few songs, after which I would preach. It was March 1986, and this was my first evangelistic crusade on foreign soil. I was pumped! We had distributed hundreds of fliers and were expecting thousands of people to show up.

But it was just not meant to be—our crusade peaked out with a grand total of seven people. Three of those were members of our Costa Rican family, which means we had four first-time visitors. Within 15 minutes, my message was finished. I had exhausted my Spanish vocabulary. The altar call was given. An already-saved grandma came forward seeking prayer for her arthritis. We prayed. She left. The meeting was over.

We were totally bummed and figured the crusade to be a failure. As we were packing up the equipment, a gang of rough-looking guys walked up to one of our workers and asked, "Where's that preacher who was talking about Jesus?"

"Why?" he asked, fearing for my life. "What do you want with him?"

"We were listening from the other side of the plaza. His story is a lot like ours. We're on drugs and involved in crime, but his words made sense to us. We're tired of this life, and we want to give our lives to the Lord. We want to get saved."

We led them to Jesus, and they became faithful followers. We later found out that they had been terrorizing the surrounding neighborhoods and people avoided them like the plague. But they attended church with us and participated in our intense prayer meetings. During the remainder of our year in Costa Rica, they became our good friends.

EXTREME PERSONAL LESSON:

**Preach the Word. The Bible clearly states
it will not return void. Don't ever be afraid
to share Jesus with others. Your presence in
their lives is temporary. His presence is eternal.
When life makes it impossible to follow up,
trust Him for the rest. He loves His
children and will care for them.**

Jeri and I were living in another culture, eating new foods and speaking another language in someone else's home. We bought our groceries at the Saturday open-air market and sat down every evening around the dinner table with our new *tica* (Costa Rican family). We had no car and depended on city buses and taxis for transportation.

Does this sound strange? Not to us. This was the great adventure. This was life with Jesus. This was the thrill of launching into the deep. This was the excitement of growing in ways we had never grown before. This was our part in the Great Commission.

Is everyone called to do what we did? Of course not. But everyone is called to obey the Lord. Whatever He has called you to do, do it with all your might. Go after it! Make your life count. Be one of those who dare to obey Christ completely.

Years later, in 1990, Jeri and I were going through some photographs and came across a picture of the converted Costa Rican gang. We wondered where they had ended up. We knew that many of them had gone on to serve the Lord, but where were they now?

We found out 10 years later during one of our Awake America crusades held in the Miami Arena in 2000. There I was, preaching the Gospel 14 years after that first crusade in Desamparados when up walked Joseph, one of the former gang members. I barely recognized him—he was clean-cut and living for God. Joseph explained how his life had been radically changed that Saturday afternoon. His family had eventually moved to Miami. Joseph took the Christ he met in Costa Rica with him, and he never turned back.

Joseph had become an extreme Christian. His life was radically changed because he dared to obey Christ completely.

**WANTED:
EXTREME
CHRISTIANS**

The Adventure of a Lifetime

CHAPTER EIGHT

EXTREME LESSON:

Obedience to God will take us places we would never have gone ourselves and allow us to do things that we could never have done ourselves.

"No eye has seen, no ear has heard, no mind has conceived what God has prepared for those who love him."

I CORINTHIANS 2:9 NIV

With a good handle on the Spanish language, Jeri and I soon found ourselves unpacking our bags in Argentina. We had finally arrived.

During our stay in Costa Rica, I had taken the time to write my testimony into a little booklet titled *I Believe in Miracles*. With the help of a professional translator, we were able to publish thousands of copies in Spanish. Since then, it has been translated into seven languages under the name *Stone Cold Heart*, and more than one million copies are in circulation. Any time we share our personal testimonies of how God turned our lives around, those stories become a powerful weapon for evangelism.

One of our favorite pastimes in Argentina was boarding one of the many commuter trains in Buenos Aires with a box of about 100 booklets. We would settle into a car and wait for it to fill with passengers. After the whistle sounded for departure, the doors would shut and the train would begin rolling down the tracks. The people would settle in for their 30-minute ride to the central station.

At an opportune time I would stand at one end of the car and loudly announce:

Hola, mi nombre es Esteban Hill. Yo era traficante y drugadicto por muchos años en los Estados Unidos. Tomaba alcohol y fumaba marijuana y comitia crimines para sustener mis habitos. Pero un dia, un hombre de Dios, me hablo del amor de Jesus. Yo quieria cambiar pero no sabia como. En ese dia Cristo me toco y me transformo. Ahora, vivo en Argentina para compartir con ustedes el amor de Jesus. Quiero regalarte una copia de mi testimonio se llama *Creo en Milagros*. Es absolutemente gratis. Si queres una copia, por favor, levante su mano. Y despues de leerlo, Jeri y yo estamos aqui para contestar tus preguntas y orar contigo. Muchas gracias!

If you were unable to understand this little Spanish dissertation, please allow me:

Hello, my name is Steve Hill. I was a drug dealer and drug addict for many years in the United States. I drank alcohol and smoked marijuana and committed crimes to support my habit. But one day a man of God spoke to me about the love of Jesus. I wanted to change but didn't know how. That day Jesus Christ touched me and transformed me. Now I live in Argentina to share with you the love of Jesus. I would like to give you a copy of my testimony called *I Believe in Miracles*. It's absolutely free. If you would like a copy, please raise your hand. After you read it, Jeri and I will be here to answer your questions and pray with you. Thank you very much.

Of course, we had a captive audience—they had to listen. There was nowhere to go. To our surprise, every single time we proclaimed the love of Jesus and offered the booklet, the majority of passengers would raise their hands. Jeri and I would distribute the books and spend the remainder of the trip talking, counseling and often leading people to Jesus.

We had our share of hecklers who despised us or the United States for our part in the Falkland War. They tried to hold me personally responsible for that disastrous time in Argentine history, but in street (or train) ministry you learn to ignore such opposition. My solution: just talk louder.

Maybe you're thinking, *Man, Steve, you're bold. I could never do anything like that.* Friend, of course you could. It's amazing what happens when you say to Jesus, "OK, Jesus, use me. I'm gonna walk over to those people and get their attention. You take over from there." It's like He puts His words in your mouth. A Holy Ghost boldness takes over. Even if you stumble over a few words, what does it matter? The most important elements of evangelism are your availability and obedience.

Whatever you do, don't be guilty of being ashamed or embarrassed about proclaiming the love of Jesus. God's Word warns, "For whoever is ashamed of Me and My words in this adulterous and sinful generation, the Son of Man will also be ashamed of him when He comes in the glory of His Father with the holy angels" (Mark 8:38).

The other day I was talking with Seth Kimbraugh, a young, professional stunt cyclist who competes in the X Games. His name is usually on anything having to do with stunt cycling. He recently placed fourth at a meet in San Francisco. The competition was fierce, and Seth gave it all he had. Of course, to most of us these stunt cyclists, with their spins, twirls, flips and jumps are nothing but fanatical daredevils—the next generation of Evel Knievels. But Seth sees it differently. He sees every new jump as a challenge and has learned to overcome fear.

"I remember when it was time to attempt my first complete flip on my cycle," he told me. "I was scared. I had never done it before. I knew how to do it, but actually doing it was a whole other story. Finally I made the decision and just did it. You know what? It was easy, almost natural. It was as if the bike became an extension of me."

When I asked him why he chose cycling, he responded, "I love the Lord with all my heart. Cycling gives me the chance to witness for Jesus. I ride for the Lord, and everywhere I go He opens doors for me to share about Him."

Wow! If Seth, who is just a normal guy, can overcome the fear of a new stunt, become one of the top cyclists in the world and share Jesus everywhere he goes, then what can God do through your life? If God could save Steve Hill, deliver him from drugs, train him in the Word, enable him to learn Spanish and put him on the mission field, why can't God mightily use you too?

So, what's the problem? Let's get radical. Let's step out and do something for Jesus. Let's smash through that fear barrier and step into the glorious realm of victory!

EXTREME PERSONAL LESSON:

God wants you to be a witness for Him, but you must be willing to open your mouth. Step out in faith and watch how He takes over.

It was now time for Jeri and me to dig in our heels and get to work in Argentina. To me, church planting is a lot like farming. First, you find a good plot of land that can produce a crop. Second, you remove any stumps, rocks or boulders—anything that could stop the plow must be dealt with.

After that, you prepare the land for the crop by turning the soil and cutting furrows for the seed. Next comes seed planting and then you wait. Every farmer will tell you—there's always the wait. Finally, it's harvest time. I believe it was Charles Finney who said, "For us not to expect a spiritual harvest of souls is the same as a farmer not expecting a physical harvest of crops." Expect a harvest!

We found an area in Buenos Aires that needed a church and joined with a local pastor interested in leading a new congregation. We bathed the vacant lot in intercessory prayer; we bound the devil and demons that had run free among the people. Remember the part about removing stumps and boulders? I liken that to binding the demons hindering the harvest. Next, we planted our seeds by handing out fliers and putting up a banner that proclaimed "Jesus Saves & Heals." Finally it was time to set up sound equipment and begin holding services.

Another congregation from a neighboring town came to help us draw in the people. We worshipped the Lord, preached the Word, cast out devils and prayed for the sick. Within a few months, there was a thriving congregation of new believers.

Sound simple? It's not. The great Argentine evangelist Carlos Anacondia calls it "bustin' rocks and gettin' dirty." Church planting is some of the hardest work you'll ever do.

While I was actively involved in this local crusade, God had given Jeri a different assignment. She was on a crusade of her own. Across the street from our crusade site was a small kiosk. These stores were tiny but crammed with most of the neighborhood's basic necessities. A well-located, popular kiosk can make the owner a good living.

The owner of this kiosk was Norma, a young woman who claimed to be an Argentine revolutionist and who was extremely comfortable with any kind of confrontation. She was living above the little store with her boyfriend.

Each night, while I was at the crusade, Jeri would slip out of the meeting, cross the street and begin witnessing to the owners. Norma's boyfriend soon made it a habit of escaping Jeri's bold witness, leaving Norma alone. Between customers, Jeri would flood Norma with the love of the Lord. In turn, Norma would pelt Jeri with questions, anything to sidetrack my determined wife.

This went on for three months. If you had ventured into this kiosk during this time, you would've found an on-fire woman of God patiently waiting to confront a stubborn agnostic with all the answers. Often, when we drove home from the crusade in our car, I'd listen to my wife's cries as she prayed over Norma's soul. She would then pour out her heart to me. "She's so hard, Steve. She's so cold. Am I wasting my time? Is she ever going to get saved?"

I reminded Jeri of one of our favorite Bible verses, Psalm 126:6 (*NIV*): "He who goes out weeping, carrying seed to sow, will return with songs of joy, carrying sheaves with him." "That's a promise, Jeri," I said. "Besides, don't ever forget how hard you were before you got saved."

By the way, my friend, this verse says that we must go forth weeping. Many Christian workers fail to incorporate the most important ingredient in evangelism: tears. Your tears will often be used by God to soften the hard soul of a sinner's heart. Weep for the lost!

Jeri reflected back on her own life, before she had met Christ. Her mom had been raped when she was just 17 years old—Jeri was born nine months later. As a little girl growing up in North Dakota, she longed for a father. Her fondest memories were those of her Norwegian granddad who loved her as his own. Her teenage years brought nothing but pain. She grew up with a loving mom but a violent, alcoholic stepfather. She got into drugs and drifted deep into the party lifestyle. Eventually Jeri was arrested for selling drugs. She hated life and couldn't imagine a future with any promise. She only envisioned more drugs, more alcohol, more fighting and an early grave.

One Saturday morning when Jeri was 16 years old, a pastor from a small Assembly of God church knocked on her door. Someone had told the pastor about Jeri, and he felt a special burden from the Lord for her soul. "Are you Jeri Larson?" he asked.

"Yes, and who are you?" was her cold response.

"My name is Bob. I pastor a church just down the street, and I came to tell you Jesus loves you and has a plan for your life." With that, Jeri became indignant, told him she wasn't interested and closed the door.

The next Saturday he returned with the same simple message, "Jeri, Jesus loves you and has a plan for your life." This time she was more adamant with her disinterest and slammed the door in his face.

The next Saturday he came back again and was greeted by Jeri's stepfather shouting at the top of his lungs, "If you come back to this house one more time, I'll have you arrested for trespassing!"

The next Saturday morning he was back. As a matter of fact, he came back almost every Saturday for two years. But each visit ended the same way.

The pastor's routine remained the same. He showed up every week about the same time. He had learned that most drug addicts can be found at home between eight a.m. and noon—they party all night long until the sun comes up. At the light of day they're usually back home, hung over.

One Saturday morning in October 1975, the pastor showed up at the front door and knocked. No one answered. He banged harder. Still no response. A quick look through the living room window explained why. The house was completely empty—the family had moved.

Undaunted, the pastor went home, got on his knees and cried out to Jesus. "Lord, I've been faithful to share Your love with this girl for the last two years. You see what's happened—the family moved. Since You're omnipresent, I've got just one question, Where is she?!" With that, he waited for a response.

The Lord quickly answered with a vision. The pastor saw a white house and the number of a highway. That was good enough for him, and he raced from intercession to the intersection. Turning down the highway, he could only scan the sides of the road looking for the house. He continued to pray. He had no idea where he was going, but God had a plan.

He spotted the house, turned into the driveway, slipped out of his car like he had done for the last two years, walked up to the steps, mumbling a prayer, and knocked. Jeri answered. Her jaw dropped, and she said, "How did you find me?" Without missing a beat he said, "Jeri, Jesus told me where you were because He loves you and has a plan for your life."

The battle was over. Jeri prayed with the pastor right then and there, and within two weeks she had entered the Teen Challenge program in Muskegon, Michigan. Eighteen months later she was chosen to attend Twin Oaks Academy in Lindale, Texas. You know the rest.

Friend, remembering your own testimony can be a powerful weapon. Now, with Norma's salvation on the line, it was crucial for Jeri to encourage herself in the Lord just like the psalmist had said. "I shall remember the deeds of the LORD; surely I will remember Thy wonders of old. I will meditate on all Thy work, and muse on Thy deeds" (Ps. 77:11-12).

Meditation and musing are serious spiritual exercises that can bring incredible results. This has to do with actually going back to the circumstance—feeling the pain, remembering the suffering and then reliving the experience of deliverance, healing and salvation.

Let God help you overcome your present battle by taking you back to the victories of the past. Jesus is the same yesterday, today and forever. If He healed you before, why wouldn't He heal you again? If He met your financial need before, don't you think He still cares about you now? If He can save you, why can't He save others?

EXTREME PERSONAL LESSON:

Remember how God provided for you in the past. When you meditate on His deeds, you will receive strength for your current problems.

As Jeri began to think about how hard-hearted she had been and how Jesus had gotten hold of her in spite of herself, strength welled up inside her. If God could save her, then He could save Norma.

It was the last night of the three-month crusade. Jeri had faithfully witnessed to Norma almost every night, talking with her for three to four hours each night. The clock was ticking away; it was decision time. Jeri marched into the kiosk and right up to the counter. Then she raised her fist in the air and slammed it down with righteous zeal.

Norma almost went into cardiac arrest when Jeri shouted, "Norma! I've been coming in here to your kiosk every night for three months! Jesus has changed my life, and He wants to change yours! You've heard everything I have to say about Jesus! Now, I want to know what you are going to do about it. Do you want Jesus or not?"

In shock, Norma replied, "OK, OK, I'm ready. Tell me what to do." Jeri did and Norma got saved!

She kicked her boyfriend out of the apartment and sold the little store three weeks later. She moved in with us to be discipled and several months later entered a four-year Bible school. She graduated, applied for a missions appointment to Africa and is now one of the most godly missionaries ever to set foot on that continent.

EXTREME PERSONAL LESSON:

Don't give up on your lost family, friends or neighbors. It is God's will for everyone to be saved. Keep plowing and sowing.

Our first church plant was a one-year project. With that completed and under our belt, Jeri and I were ready to tackle new territory. We visited our denomination's central office, located in Buenos Aires, Argentina, to receive our next assignment. We asked the superintendent where the Assemblies of God wanted a church. He said cautiously, "We have several areas in the frontier of Argentina that desperately need a church. Let me give you a dozen choices and you decide." My reaction was thanks, but no thanks. I pressed him, "We want to plant a church in a region of Argentina where no other missionary has gone. Where do you want a church more than anywhere else?"

We understood his hesitation; if he selected the place, he would feel responsible if things went wrong. But we were insistent.

We were seated in his office; hanging on the wall behind him was a giant, colored map of Argentina. He pointed to a spot in the desert of Neuquen. "It's called the graveyard of pastors," he said slowly. "We need a strong work in the city of Neuquen."

"OK, we'll go," was my immediate response.

He was in shock. "But you've never been there. It's hot, dusty and in the middle of nowhere."

My reply was simply, "How many people are there?"

"Over 300,000," he said.

"That's it. We'll go," I said. "God didn't call us to a certain climate or terrain—He called us to people."

A few months later Jeri and I packed our belongings in a truck and started out on the 500-mile trip from Buenos Aires down to Neuquen. It was grueling, but we made it. With the help of a dynamic Argentine pastor, Hector Ferreyra, we established a powerful church that has to date planted over 20 other churches. Now, 15 years later, Hector and I have ministered together in evangelistic crusades around the world.

EXTREME PERSONAL LESSON:

When Jesus said, "Go into all the world," that's exactly what He meant. A specific calling, such as the Macedonian vision (see Acts 16:9-10), is possible but unusual. If an area is populated with people who need to hear about Jesus, then God can mightily use you there.

The problems Jeri and I faced in Argentina are the same ones missionaries face all over the world. There's so much to do, resources are limited and workers are few. It makes for very slow progress. But thanks to dedicated churches and individuals in the United States and Canada who sent money and construction teams to help, we were able to build seven churches in Argentina.

The orphanage in San Nicolas, Argentina, was also a true miracle in the making. We visited the old facility and its director, Carlos Naranjo. We were heartsick as we toured the dilapidated building that was in desperate need of repairs yet cramped with more than 100 sweet little residents. They hovered around us, many clinging to our sides for dear life.

We saw the beginnings of a new spacious facility under construction, but it was a long way from completion. Carlos called me an angel and said our reason for being in Argentina was to help him. We wanted to, recalling what James wrote, "This is pure and undefiled religion in the sight of our God and Father, to visit orphans and widows in their distress, and to keep oneself unstained by the world" (Jas. 1:27).

Carlos desperately needed funding to complete the project, but Jeri and I were broke. Although our coffers were always empty on the mission field, we believed God could provide everything that was needed.

Later I cried out in prayer, "Jesus, my heart is right, and I'm keeping myself unstained from the evils of this world. Please, Lord Jesus, help us help these children. They're fatherless and motherless—they have nothing. They deserve a decent roof over their heads, food and a good night's sleep. Please, Jesus, send the funds."

His answer was clear, "Bring My people to see the need and they will respond."

But how?

Unknown to us, God was raising up a man in the United States, Johnny Brown, with a burden to help us. He began bringing U.S. pastors to Argentina, and they, in turn, brought back teams of workers from their own churches. Funds started flowing in, and the orphanage was completed within a matter of months. God even sent a team of women to paint, hang curtains and decorate the rooms. To our amazement, an Argentine hamburger chain donated kitchen appliances and cafeteria furniture. All this was done because we stepped out and trusted God, which brings me to a powerful truth.

EXTREME PERSONAL LESSON:

God is looking for those who will step out in faith and trust Him. When we do, He will provide in ways we never thought of.

I feel such excitement as I write these words. I sense faith rising up in your heart. Friend, you can accomplish great things for God! Remember, "No eye has seen, no ear has heard, no mind has conceived what God has prepared for those who love him" (1 Cor. 2:9, *NIV*).

Another of my all-time favorite verses is "My God shall supply all your needs according to His riches in glory in Christ Jesus" (Phil. 4:19).

The Christian life is a wonderful adventure. Let Him take you places you never dreamed of. Let Him work through you. Be an instrument of His love. He has great plans for those who dare to obey Him completely.

WANTED: EXTREME CHRISTIANS

Feeding the Fire

CHAPTER NINE

EXTREME LESSON:

We must pay close attention to the fire
in our own souls, for the natural tendency
of a fire is to die out.

─────────

*"And for this reason I remind you to kindle afresh the gift of God
which is in you through the laying on of my hands."*

II TIMOTHY 1:6

It was 1991 and we were thoroughly enjoying our life of ministry in Neuquen, Argentina. That's why I was so surprised when I realized I was going through a spiritual drought. All I can say is that with great victories often come great battles. I found myself crying out to God, "I feel so empty, Lord. My heart is like a desert wasteland. Where are You? Don't leave me. What do I have to do to feel Your presence again? Don't take your Holy Spirit from me." He seemed nowhere to be found.

I remembered back to May 1979, 12 years earlier, when David Wilkerson warned us of times like this during a sermon he gave at our graduation from Twin Oaks Academy. Jeri and I had absorbed every word of his sermon that day.

Wilkerson's message that day, "Thou Shalt Have Spells," had stayed with me. "Right now," he had told us, "you are on top of the world. You're graduating from the academy. You've completed this leg of the race. But oh, my friend, there are battles ahead. Of course, you will relish great victories, but you will also pass through dark valleys. You will experience times of blistering spiritual drought. Your tongue will be parched. You will crave a drop of water from heaven but will feel nothing. You will cry out to God and hear no response."

Most of the students were in shock. We had been expecting a more encouraging word, a victory theme, a charge to the troops. Instead, David poured out his heart and gave us a glimpse of his personal voyage. He shared about preaching in crusades when the Spirit of the Lord seemed miles away. He spoke of demonic attacks when the kingdom of darkness seemed to be winning. I savored every word.

Yes, down the road you will pass through dry, desert times. You will feel as if the Lord has left you. But always remember, He is there. The Bible says in Hebrews 13:5 that He will never leave you nor forsake you.

He instructs us in Isaiah 43:1-3, "Do not fear, for I have redeemed you; I have called you by name; you are Mine! When you pass through the waters, I will be with you; and through the rivers, they will not overflow you. When you walk through the fire, you will not be scorched, nor will the flame burn you. For I am the LORD your God."

The Lord continues to speak to the parched pilgrim in Isaiah 44:3, "For I will pour out water on the thirsty land and streams on the dry ground."

As I cried my heart out 12 years later, that message was like a lighthouse by a raging sea. I felt so alone. Here I was in the midst of the mighty Argentine revival, yet I felt so empty. How could this be? What was the Lord doing? The man others viewed as a spiritual giant felt like a lost child.

I cry as I write these words, because even today I can still feel that debilitating emptiness and know it's something other people go through too. Perhaps you're caught in the middle of a deep, dark trial and feel as if everyone, including God, has forsaken you. You pray, but you don't sense His presence. You read His Word, but it doesn't spark anything. You desire the sweet presence of God, but all you feel is loneliness.

I firmly believe the Lord would say to you, "I am with you. I have redeemed you. I have purchased you. You are My property. I take care of My own. You will pass through to the other side. Trust Me!"

EXTREME PERSONAL LESSON:

God's promises are not subject to our present conditions. His Word stands true regardless of our circumstances.

I realized God was calling me to His side because He was about to do a new thing. He was about to show up in ways I had not yet experienced. But I wasn't ready—I needed to go deeper in my walk with Him.

I began starting each day in the early morning hours locked in my study to spend time on my knees in prayer and in the Word. I began soaking myself in the writings of the great Puritan pastors and teachers, revivalists of years gone by. I began crying out, "Jesus, do it again!" God kept calling me to go deeper. Fasting for extended periods of time became part of my normal routine.

God was doing a new work in me. I wrote in my journal:

I have discovered once again the necessity of spending time with Him. As I read His Word, as I devour great books about Him, as I study the marvelous exploits achieved through Him, it's as if everything material— even the ministry itself—dims in comparison. There's no greater comfort. There's no greater joy. The desire for these things to disappear and become what they really are has come to pass by the very action of seeking Him. Holy Spirit, You've been working on me. Teach me, Teacher.

The words of the holy Scottish pastor Robert Murray McCheyne made perfect sense to me, "A calm hour with God is worth a whole lifetime with man."

I began experiencing visitations from God that continue to this day. At times I sense His nearness as I quietly sit alone in my study. Other times His Word comes alive as if He were audibly speaking to me. I don't know how else to express this experience, but I can vividly feel His presence, His favor.

He began to manifest His presence at our crusades with a mighty outpouring of His Holy Spirit. People would weep uncontrollably during the services. Drug addicts were set free as they called out to the only One who could deliver them. Sinners were convicted of sin as they sensed the holiness of Jesus. The presence of God could be felt in a way that caused even the strongest to melt. During outside meetings, people were riveted as if their shoes were nailed to the pavement, and tears flowed down their faces. The love of Jesus was melting hearts, changing lives.

During a crusade in 1991, at a city park in Curico, Chile, the presence of God fell in a powerful yet unusual way. While preaching, I noticed some cars pulling off to the side of the street so the drivers could watch what was going on. *How strange,* I thought. *God must be up to something.* I turned over the service to someone else and walked over to investigate. The drivers were sitting in silence with stunned looks on their faces.

I would tap on the windows of car after car and ask, "Why did you stop?" One driver said, "I don't know. I just feel something."

"May I join you?" I replied. "I'm a minister of the Gospel, and I know what's happening."

I would sit with them in their car and explain the love of Jesus and the need for repentance. I would then lead them to the Lord, and inevitably they would start crying uncontrollably as God's presence saturated them.

This was something new for me, and the experience would spoil me forever. I'd rather have the presence of God in my meetings than a hundred of the finest theologians.

EXTREME PERSONAL LESSON:

God's presence is all we need. Everything else fades as we see our life and ministry from heaven's perspective.

The Lord began opening doors of ministry for us all over the world. We finished our work in Neuquen, and later that year the Assemblies of God Division of Foreign Missions gave me the title "missionary evangelist."

I was invited to hold crusades in Uruguay, Colombia, Spain and Russia. To raise funds for these crusades, we decided to relocate our offices to the United States. By this time, God had blessed us with two beautiful children, Ryan and Shelby. Once again, we put an ad in the paper and a sign in front of our home. Once again we sold out to the bare walls.

We flew into Miami from Buenos Aires; and by the time our plane landed, I had asked the Lord for just one favor: *Please arrange for us to live in Lindale, Texas, the home of evangelist/ author Leonard Ravenhill.* Leonard's best-known book, *Why Revival Tarries,* had been used by God to build an unquenchable desire in my heart for Holy Ghost revival. I deeply desired to be mentored by this great man of God. He was in his 80s, so I knew it was now or never.

The Lord began opening doors. David Wilkerson said we could live in one of his duplexes in Lindale, just two miles from Leonard's home. The moment we arrived in Lindale, even before unpacking, I called information for his phone number.

With trembling hands, I began to dial. Leonard answered in his British accent, "Hello." I was tongue-tied. "Who is it?" he added. *Say something! Say anything!* "My name is Steve Hill," I said, finally finding my voice. "I'm a missionary evangelist and just moved into the area. David Wilkerson has given us a home to live in." (I figured mentioning Wilkerson would be an advantage since he and David were good friends.) "I wonder if it would be possible to spend some time with you." His answer was abrupt, "Tonight, seven o'clock."

I can't believe what I said next. "Brother Ravenhill, my wife and I just arrived after driving 12 hours. We're exhausted. Could we make it for another night?"

"Call me later," he said. *Click!* I couldn't believe it. He hung up on me—he didn't even say good-bye.

I turned to Jeri. "Honey," I said, "you're not going to believe what just happened. Leonard Ravenhill hung up on me, just because I said I was tired. He can't do that! I know he's a man of God, but so am I."

With that, I grabbed the phone and redialed the number. He answered, not "Hello," but "Yes?"

"Brother Ravenhill, it's Steve Hill again. Tonight will be fine. I'll be there at seven o'clock sharp." He muttered something and hung up. "He did it again!" I told Jeri.

I was at his door at 6:59 p.m. I knocked, waited a few seconds, heard someone coming and thought I was going to faint. I was prepared for a prophet of God to swing open the door, scream out, "Yea, I say unto you!" and slam the door in my face. Instead, a humble but stern-looking man opened the door and shoved a small index card in my face. On it was written, "A man who is intimate with God will never be intimidated by men."

I couldn't believe this guy. "You tricked me!" I said. "You hung up on me on purpose. You were testing me to see what I was made of, to find out if a few abrupt words would chase me away."

He chuckled, "That's right, son, and you passed the test. Come in."

The hours Brother Ravenhill and I spent together over the next several years left a deep impression on my heart. Leonard's words always pointed me to Jesus. He would say things like, "Remember, Stevie, God wants to reveal His mysteries to you, but He won't holler His secrets." Or, "Make sure what you're doing is of the Lord. You'll be judged by fire. Everything that is not of God will be burned up. You don't want to stand knee-deep in ashes on Judgment Day."

His dear wife, Martha, always had a batch of warm home-made cookies and a cup of hot English tea waiting. I would tell her that she could make an incredible living by marketing her recipes. She always received my compliments graciously.

I found ways to serve the Ravenhills. Mowing their lawn, helping Leonard obtain a visa to visit Ireland, painting the two white lions at the entrance to their home, cleaning leaves out of their gutters or trimming the bushes—it was all a joy. I felt as "spiritual" cleaning the gutters as I did preaching the Gospel. These were precious saints of God, and I counted it a blessing to do anything for them.

EXTREME PERSONAL LESSON:

Honor those to whom honor is due. Glean spiritual truths from pioneers who've gone before you. Their experiences can enrich your life and help guide you into maturity.

In 1992 I had just completed writing a devotional Bible guide titled *On Earth As It Is in Heaven*. The guide was ready for publication, and I asked Leonard to look over it. I was waiting for the right opportunity to ask for his endorsement. He was thrilled to see that I was a student of revival and a collector of classic Christian books.

Later, he came over to my house and blessed my study. I had the publisher place Leonard's endorsement on the back cover of the devotional. He wrote: "In my long life I have seen many publications of daily Bible reading by Robert Murray McCheyne. But this by Stephen Hill is by far the best, supported as it is by choice classic utterances from great historic preachers."

My dear friend died of a stroke in 1994 at the age of 86. He is buried in Garden Valley, Texas, just a few feet from Keith Green.

On his tombstone are these words: "Are the things you are living for worth Christ dying for?"

It's strange, but I can still hear his voice.

His wonderful wife, Martha, went on to be with Jesus in the fall of 2001. I have a feeling heaven celebrated their homecoming.

EXTREME PERSONAL LESSON:

The legacy you leave, either good or bad, will speak volumes after you're gone. Live a holy, consecrated life.

Leonard Ravenhill was instrumental in shaping the lives of thousands of ministers, mine included. He never wavered from his God-given message and always linked the words "revival" and "holiness" together in the same breath. He spoke often of the unction of the Holy Spirit and encouraged everyone to stay on fire for Jesus. His legacy will endure for eternity.

The influence we have on others, the legacy we leave behind, is so important that I've dedicated an entire chapter at the end of the book to this topic. I trust you will be challenged like never before to make a positive difference with your life.

As Jeri and I continued holding crusades in the United States and abroad, we were witnessing an incredible harvest of souls. My life had been radically rejuvenated, and the results of the crusades were unlike anything I had ever experienced before.

In 1992, we met up with Milton, a 17-year-old from Palmira, Colombia, who was trapped in a whirlwind lifestyle of violence and gangs. His father had been an assassin for the mafia. When Milton was just a child, his dad showed him a bullet and said, "Milton, one day you're going to kill people, just like me."

Shortly thereafter, his dad was killed by another assassin's bullet. From that time on, Milton had one desire: to be a killer just like his dad. He wanted to fill his dad's shoes, but God had a different plan.

We met Milton the night he wandered by our crusade tent and stopped to listen to my message on God's love. I saw him in the back of the tent and hollered out that Jesus loved him and had a plan for his life. He was soon at the altar, tears flowing as he accepted Christ into his life.

Bitterness and hatred disappeared. The pain of his past gave way to the healing power of Jesus. Milton grew quickly in the Lord and eventually moved to the United States with his family. Jeri and I were so encouraged with his growth that we sent him to Christ for the Nations Institute in Dallas, Texas, and then later to the Brownsville Revival School of Ministry in Pensacola, Florida.

One day he asked if he could change his last name to Hill since I had become like a father to him. My response was that he had become like family to me. Today he calls me "Dad" and I call him "son." Milton Hill and his wife, Brooke, have worked in the mission field, leading hundreds of souls to Jesus. They now work alongside Jeri and me and are following the call of God on their lives. What a God we serve!

EXTREME PERSONAL LESSON:

The power of the Cross can change anyone. The Bible says God doesn't want anyone to perish. Don't limit Him when it comes to the salvation of the hardest sinner.

Our children, Ryan and Shelby, were growing up and experiencing firsthand what made Mommy and Daddy tick. All we cared about (besides our children, of course!) was souls, and we were willing to do anything and go anywhere for Jesus. At an earlier time in my life I had criss-crossed the country in futile attempts to "find myself"; now I was criss-crossing the globe to help others find God.

In 1994, we were led to help plant a church in Russia. By then, Ryan and Shelby weren't surprised when we loaded them and some of our belongings on a plane and moved to Belarus. After we arrived, we began holding crusades in a local cultural center and in open-air venues. People flocked to hear the pure Word of God.

During one of these crusades, a drug addict screamed out in Russian (our interpreter translated), "What are you now going to do? Leave me in this condition?" The next day I visited him at his home where he asked me the same question. My heart sank. He was right. I thought of James 2:15-17, "If a brother or sister is without clothing and in need of daily food, and one of you says to them, 'Go in peace, be warmed and be filled,' and yet you do not give them what is necessary for their body, what use is that? Even so faith, if it has no works, is dead, being by itself."

I later went back to the facility we had been using and gathered together our two dozen or so workers. Some of them were from the States and others were from the local Russian church. I told them how we had to do something for the Russian people trapped in alcohol and drug addiction.

From that came the beginnings of a Teen Challenge center that flourishes to this day. It is located in Baranovichi, Belarus, and is staffed by local believers. Its financial support comes from Russian churches, our ministry and private individuals. The center also supports itself by growing its own food and selling crafts and goods made by its residents.

EXTREME PERSONAL LESSON:

A true Christian is motivated by Christ's love and sees needs differently from the way others do. When we see others through the eyes of Christ, our compassion for people requires that we suffer with them.

The Russian people were going through a very difficult time in their nation. In 1994, the most basic items in the States were luxuries in Russia. At times Jeri had to wait in line for a loaf of bread, once for two hours. A bag of sugar was like a bag of gold. Living conditions were rough, but the spiritual condition was marvelous. People were ripe for revival and, within a few short months, a new church had been planted.

I thank God for the strong soldiers who worked alongside us. One of them, Larry Art, had a deep interest in this new church and helped train the believers. Together we planned more crusades for the country. Posters and fliers were printed up. Over 100,000 Russian copies of *Stone Cold Heart* were ready for distribution. We were anxious to reap the next glorious harvest.

But about this time our visas were about to run out, and we couldn't keep extending them. We also needed more funding and realized it was best to base our operations for this project in the United States. So Jeri and I decided to move back to Lindale.

Back in the United States, we got involved in church crusades, missions conventions and the planning of evangelistic campaigns around the world. God's hand was everywhere; He even blessed us with a new baby girl, Kelsey, who was born in 1995. We bought another home and settled in with our three wonderful children. Life was looking normal. From our new home in Texas we would reach out around the world.

Little did we know God had another plan—something far beyond our dreams or expectations.

On Father's Day 1995, I was a guest speaker at Brownsville Assembly of God in Pensacola, Florida. Because of a busy schedule, I could stay only one day, or so I thought. Like Isaiah says of God's agenda, "'For My thoughts are not your thoughts, neither are your ways My ways,' declares the LORD. 'For as the heavens are higher than the earth, so are My ways higher than your ways, and My thoughts than your thoughts'" (Isa. 55:8-9).

As a matter of fact, everything I had planned for the next five years was about to be wiped off my itinerary. It was time for the greatest challenge I had ever known. God was ready to use those of us who dared to trust Him completely.

**WANTED:
EXTREME
CHRISTIANS**

Making Room for Revival

CHAPTER TEN

EXTREME LESSON:

There are seasons in our lives when the supernatural takes over. When this happens, be ready to make room for revival.

"So then, those who had received his word were baptized; and there were added that day about three thousand souls. And they were continually devoting themselves to the apostles' teaching and to fellowship, to the breaking of bread and to prayer. And everyone kept feeling a sense of awe; and many wonders and signs were taking place through the apostles. And all those who had believed were together, and had all things in common; and they began selling their property and possessions, and were sharing them with all, as anyone might have need."

ACTS: 2: 41-45

This chapter isn't meant to frighten anyone, but it might. You see, many people are afraid of the call of God. They fear that Jesus might really and truly take over their lives and call them to difficult tasks. The thought of going somewhere new, meeting strangers and having to publicly proclaim His message totally freaks them out. They live in terror of this heavenly prospect.

The same is true of revival. Many people freak out at the mention of the word. They get nauseated at the mere taste of something new and different touching their spiritual palate.

But think about it this way. If you're going to have a house-guest, you adjust your lifestyle to accommodate him. You prepare a room for her to sleep in, maybe putting the kids together in one room. You set another place at mealtime. You modify what you wear around the house—no more walking around in skivvies. The list goes on.

Just as you prepare for a visit from your friend, you must also prepare for a visitation from The Friend. True revival will change you and your church—forever!

Ask a dedicated soldier about the intensity of his military preparation and he'll say, "War is what I'm trained for. I'm a soldier and this is what soldiers do." Spiritually speaking, revival is what Christians should be trained for; it's what Christians must do.

The Bible gives us a phenomenal view of true Holy Ghost revival. The move of God in the book of Acts changed everything. Tongues of fire fell from heaven, and the disciples and others were filled with the Holy Ghost. It was unlike anything they had ever experienced. *That's revival!*

What was the next step? According to the Word of God, they didn't sit around and become spiritually fat. They left the building and went out into the world. *That's revival!*

Nonbelievers were astonished at the signs and wonders. *That's revival!* The disciples were criticized for these manifestations. They were ridiculed for the way they were acting. *That's revival!* Rather than focusing on the criticism, Peter took the disciples on a journey to Christ. *That's revival!*

Repentance was preached. *That's revival!* We find the early church growing from a handful of believers to more than 8,000 in a very short period of time. *That's revival!* The pains of spiritual childbirth were being felt by all. New believers had to be cared for and nurtured. *That's revival!* The poor had to be taken care of, and the spiritually hungry had to be fed. *That's revival!*

People began to share. *That's revival!* Their time was no longer their own. They were constantly in church worshiping God, partaking of Communion, listening to God's Word and watching more souls being added to their number. *That's revival!*

Let's talk about making room for revival. Revival is all about change. Leonard Ravenhill once said to me, "The reason America has not experienced widespread revival is because we're content to live without it." I add that another reason is because we don't want to change. We love our lifestyle and don't want anyone to upset it.

Well, folks, one thing we can be certain of in life is change. As a matter of fact, the oxymoron "constant change" is actually a definitive characteristic of revival. Revival brings church growth, and the congregation must adjust to new faces and new challenges. But the greatest challenge in revival has to do with our own spiritual condition. We say we want revival, but spiritually many of us are not ready to accept it.

Have you ever heard anyone say, "That person has God in a box"? They're talking about limiting God, but think about it: Can you imagine God in a box? Impossible! My friend, *we're* the ones in the box. We're the ones trapped within the confines of our own limited understanding. God is free!

Revival is all about change, and spiritual change is often the hardest. Why? Because many of us feel that we already have a handle on our spiritual lives. We love God, we're in His Word, we're praying, we seek His face, we work—what more is there? But some of us are so cautious that we've become calloused. We're so careful about how we grow that we've actually stunted our spiritual growth.

We need to be as open to change as Apollos was in Acts 18:24-28. The Bible says that he was fervent in spirit, instructed in the way of the Lord and mighty in the Scriptures. Sound spiritual? But read what happened. He was pulled aside by Aquila and Priscilla, heard how to go deeper in God and responded. Rather than saying something like, "Who do you two think you are? I'm Apollos. I have a following. I'm mightily used of God," he responded humbly and his ministry grew. He made room for revival. Read this marvelous story for yourself.

According to Acts 19:1-7, Paul once encountered a group of disciples who were following God, but apparently they had not yet arrived at their spiritual destination. Paul talked to them about the Holy Ghost; then they opened up and received a powerful infilling. They could have said "We're floating along just fine, thank you. We don't need you to come along and rock our boat." Instead, my friend, they received this new spiritual teaching, and it changed their lives forever. They made room for revival. Read it for yourself.

Friend, open up and allow the Holy Spirit to take you farther in Christ than you've ever gone before.

EXTREME PERSONAL LESSON:

We are called to change and to never stop learning. When the Lord challenges you to grow, don't shrink back in fear. He wants to take you places, spiritually, where you have never been before.

It was 1984 when God started preparing me spiritually for revival—a full decade before it happened. Jeri and I were in Argentina and had been involved in ministry for almost 10 years. God had been using us to cast out demons, pray healing for the sick and bring salvation to the lost. We were on-fire disciples for Christ—and lovin' it.

Jesus lived in us and was flowing through our lives. We considered ourselves spiritual people, but God was about to show us much more!

We were thrilled when a friend invited us to attend one of the mighty evangelistic crusades of Carlos Anacondia. These crusades were marked by incredible healings and deliverances from demons.

Upon arriving, we met Carlos who, after hearing about my deliverance from drugs, asked me to share with the crowd what God had done. I jumped at the opportunity. The crowd numbered around 15,000 when I climbed up the stairs to the platform. (This was prior to my language-school training, so I had to use an interpreter.) Their roar of approval as my testimony was shared was invigorating. As a matter of fact, it was overwhelming. The crowd was pumped and filled the air with applause and praise to God.

After I had finished and as I stepped off the platform, a lady rushed up to me, grabbed my hand and put it on her forehead. She used my hand to lay hands on herself. Immediately she fell to the ground and lay motionless.

When others saw this, they ran forward, grabbing my clothes, my arms and my legs. I began laying hands on as many hungry souls as I could. People fell everywhere. It was chaotic. A surge of spiritual energy swept through me like a raging river. I was ready to take on the biggest devil in hell—*bring me the paralyzed, the blind, the deaf!* I felt it was my finest hour, so to speak.

About 10 minutes into this pandemonium, the crusade chairman came over and, through my interpreter, said, "You're causing a disturbance. This is not the time to pray for people, we'll do that later. Now is the time for the preaching of the Word of God." "Besides," he added, "a child could do what you're doing. The reason all these people are responding to you is because they saw you on the platform. They're hungry for a miracle and they think you're the man of God. Now, we would appreciate it if you would stop what you're doing. Brother Anacondia is going to preach the Word."

Sound humbling? His words sure burst my bubble. But God was starting a new chapter in my spiritual life. He was about to show me how far beyond the natural revival is. How His Spirit is able to change lives without my help. How demons scream in horror at the sound of Jesus' name—without anyone even touching those who were possessed.

As a matter of fact, that night and every night in the Anacondia crusades, we saw thousands of demon-possessed people delivered. From the platform, Carlos bound demons and devils. Screams for mercy and cries for deliverance were heard throughout the crowd. Those possessed with devils would be carted off by ushers and carried into the "demon tent." Under this yellow and white canopy, untold miracles would occur. The possessed and oppressed were set free by the power of Jesus' name.

Yes, true revival is much bigger than anything we can imagine. We must be prepared to get out of the way and let God be God. I had become stunted in my spiritual growth, and He was about to increase my stature.

EXTREME PERSONAL LESSON:

When Jesus Christ is lifted up, He will draw all men unto Himself. When God begins to move in your community, regardless how He is using you, always remember: It's all about Him.

That night and every night for several weeks at the Annacondia crusades, thousands of people ran to the altar in repentance. God was teaching me some valuable spiritual lessons, one of which was the priority of preaching His Word. Carlos always preached a simple message. He never tried to impress people with his eloquence.

Like the apostle Paul, Carlos went to them, not with lofty words, but in demonstration of power. Paul writes in 1 Corinthians 2:2-5,

> For I determined to know nothing among you except Jesus Christ, and Him crucified. And I was with you in weakness and in fear and in much trembling. And my message and my preaching were not in persuasive words of wisdom, but in demonstration of the Spirit and of power, that your faith should not rest on the wisdom of men, but on the power of God.

Like Billy Graham, Anacondia made the Cross clearly understood and repentance mandatory. The result? Millions responded to the Gospel through his ministry.

People must hear about Jesus and be given an opportunity to respond to Him. That's why, years later, anyone attending the Pensacola revival would always hear about repentance. That's why on Friday nights the baptismal pool would be full of former backsliders and newly saved sinners.

We must set aside time for the supernatural in crusade and revival meetings. One of the secrets to the longevity of the Argentine revival is that there is always time for the Lord to do a deep work in the lives of attendees. But if you want God to *spend time* with you, first *make time* for Him.

In Argentina I began craving more of the anointing of God. I learned that God has bestowed spiritual gifts on others and that we can learn from them. Of course, there must be a depth in our personal walk with God that consists of prayer, study and fasting, but we must be willing to receive from others too. Just as Paul laid his hands on Timothy, I was always eager to have great men and women of God lay hands on me.

One of my first requests of Carlos was for personal prayer. One night, right outside the demon tent, Carlos placed his hands on my forehead. I promptly fell in the mud under the power of God. What a glorious experience!

Many years later, prior to the Brownsville Revival, I requested prayer from another anointed servant of God, Sandy Millar, the Anglican vicar at Holy Trinity Brompton Church in London, England. There people were being undeniably touched by a fresh wind of the Spirit through Sandy's ministry. I was no exception.

The days, weeks, months and years ahead were a swirl of spiritual activity. Brownsville pastor John Kilpatrick and his congregation made room for revival. Lindell Cooley, their worship leader, opened up to the new sounds of revival.

The move of God at Brownsville Assembly attracted millions from around the world. The hunger for more of Jesus was made evident by their willingness to stand in long lines under the hot Florida sun, waiting to get in for that evening's service. These people were anxious to receive a fresh touch from the Lord. They were not disappointed.

How about you? Can you honestly say you have made room and are ready to see God do something new—even if it's unusual? Are you willing to make a place at the table for Jesus? Are you ready for revival? Are you another Apollos, open to the Spirit? Do you dare to obey Christ completely?

**WANTED:
EXTREME
CHRISTIANS**

Look What the Lord Has Done

CHAPTER ELEVEN

EXTREME LESSON:

God's ways of dealing with man are often far beyond our reason, logic and understanding.

"This is the LORD's doing; it is marvelous in our eyes."

PSALM 118:23

Why do so many Christians have such a difficult time accepting the fact that Jesus is touching people *today*? Why does it disturb them so when they hear things like, "Man, God really touched me during church last night"; "I felt the power of God sweep through me"; "I was delivered from my craving for cigarettes"?

Why can't today's Church accept that the God of past generations is the God of this generation? If He touched people throughout the Bible—no one argues with that—why is it so unusual to believe He's touching lives today? Why do folks work themselves into such a frenzy when they hear that someone had a powerful encounter with the Holy Ghost?

I remember the first time I read about Charles Finney's encounter with such power when he had a visitation from God. He said it was like jolts of electricity flowing through his body. Read it for yourself in Finney's journals. Why is it that over 100 years ago this great man of God experienced and wrote about this encounter, and people today have no trouble accepting it? But talk about the same thing happening today and you're greeted with raised eyebrows, skepticism and even persecution.

Friend, let me take you on a little adventure. Let's visit a man in the New Testament who had an unexpected visitation from God, and then we'll look at a few recent experiences as well, all of which resulted in life-changing conversions. You can decide for yourself whether or not they're credible.

We find Saul of Tarsus in Acts 7 so adamantly opposed to the spread of Christianity that he consented to the stoning death of Stephen.

> But they cried out with a loud voice, and covered their ears, and they rushed upon him [Stephen] with one impulse. And when they had driven him out of the city,

they began stoning him, and the witnesses laid aside their robes at the feet of a young man named Saul. And they went on stoning Stephen as he called upon the Lord and said, "Lord Jesus, receive my spirit!" (Acts 7:57-59).

In Acts 9 Saul is preparing for his trip to Damascus. With fire in his eyes, he is out to hunt down and imprison any Christians he can find.

Now Saul, still breathing threats and murder against the disciples of the Lord, went to the high priest, and asked for letters from him to the synagogues at Damascus, so that if he found any belonging to the Way, both men and women, he might bring them bound to Jerusalem (Acts 9:1-2).

It's safe to say he wasn't too big on the Gospel. But God had a plan—an extremely unconventional one—and it radically and permanently changed Saul's life.

It was broad daylight when Saul set out for Damascus and a bright light appeared out of the heavens. He would later describe it to King Agrippa as being brighter than the sun. He recalled,

While thus engaged as I was journeying to Damascus with the authority and commission of the chief priests, at midday, O King, I saw on the way a light from heaven, brighter than the sun, shining all around me and those who were journeying with me (Acts 26:12-13).

That's strange! That's one bright light! And when he saw it, he literally bit the dust. Saul fell to the ground and heard a voice saying to him,

"Saul, Saul, why are you persecuting Me?" And he [Saul]

said, "Who art Thou, Lord?" And He said, "I am Jesus whom you are persecuting, but rise, and enter the city, and it shall be told you what you must do." And the men who traveled with him stood speechless, hearing the voice, but seeing no one (Acts 9:4-7).

That's strange! Within moments, darkness enveloped Saul. Does that mean he was blinded by God?

And Saul got up from the ground, and though his eyes were open, he could see nothing; and leading him by the hand, they brought him into Damascus (Acts 9:8).

He was led to a home in Damascus where he lived in total darkness for three days. "And he was three days without sight, and neither ate nor drank" (Acts 9:9). *That's strange!*

On the third day a man named Ananias, who had received instructions from God in a vision, came and laid hands on Saul. He received his sight—but wait—there's more! During the prayer something like scales fell from his eyes!

Ananias departed and entered the house, and after laying his hands on him said, "Brother Saul, the Lord Jesus, who appeared to you on the road by which you were coming, has sent me so that you may regain your sight, and be filled with the Holy Spirit." And immediately there fell from his eyes something like scales, and he regained his sight, and he arose and was baptized (Acts 9:17-18).

That's strange! Saul of Tarsus became an on-fire believer known as Paul the Apostle and was mightily used of God. He preached the Gospel throughout the land and wrote most of the New Testament.

EXTREME PERSONAL LESSON:

**Many folks like to say that the Holy Spirit is a
perfect gentleman. After studying this story, they
might want to rethink that theology. It looks like God
can do whatever He wants, to whomever
He wants, whenever He wants.**

I often wonder what Saul did with those scales. Did he let
them fall to the floor to be swept up with the day's dirt? Did he
scoop them up and stuff them in his pocket? Regardless of what
he did, the truth remains that he was blinded by God and something like scales fell from his eyes.

If Paul were alive today and going from church to church
sharing his testimony, I wonder how many Christians would dis-
miss his story as bogus? After all, it sure is strange.

The bottom line? Some people are just like Saul of Tarsus.
They need a violent encounter with God. If you hand them a
tract, they'll throw it on the ground. They need a divine event
that grabs their attention and alters the course of their lives.

They're like the Philippian jailer in Acts 16:26-34. They need
an earthquake to get them saved.

> Suddenly there came a great earthquake, so that the foun-
> dations of the prison house were shaken; and immediate-
> ly all the doors were opened, and everyone's chains were
> unfastened. And when the jailer had been roused out of
> sleep and had seen the prison doors opened, he drew his
> sword and was about to kill himself, supposing that the
> prisoners had escaped. But Paul cried out with a loud
> voice, saying, "Do yourself no harm, for we are all here!"

And he called for lights and rushed in and, trembling with fear, he fell down before Paul and Silas, and after he brought them out, he said, "Sirs, what must I do to be saved?" And they said, "Believe in the Lord Jesus, and you shall be saved, you and your household."

And they spoke the word of the Lord to him together with all who were in his house. And he took them that very hour of the night and washed their wounds, and immediately he was baptized, he and all his household. And he brought them into his house and set food before them, and rejoiced greatly, having believed in God with his whole household.

There were others who came to Jesus calmly. They heard His message, fell under conviction and their entire "emotional outburst" consisted of a few tears. They walked down to the altar where they committed their lives to Jesus and lived faithfully for Him from then on.

Take Lydia, a businesswoman in Acts, who heard the Word and believed. No earthquake. No lightning bolt from heaven. No blindness or scales falling from her eyes.

And a certain woman named Lydia, from the city of Thyatira, a seller of purple fabrics, a worshiper of God, was listening; and the Lord opened her heart to respond to the things spoken by Paul (Acts 16:14).

EXTREME PERSONAL LESSON:

**God deals with people differently.
Be careful not to criticize the method,
and wait patiently for the results.**

For a more recent example, how about the mixed-up life of Elizabeth, a rebellious teenager from Pensacola, Florida? She came to the Brownsville Revival in 1995, was almost pushed to the altar for prayer, had hands laid on her and immediately fell into a visionary state. For two hours she had a vision of Jesus during which, she says, she was lifted into the heavenlies.

She was then literally carried around for two or three weeks, speaking prophetically and delivering words that only God could have given her. This formerly hard-drinking teen was transformed into a devoted follower of Jesus Christ. Now, over four years later, she's not only living for God but also has graduated from Bible school, married one of Pastor Kilpatrick's sons and serves in the ministry.

Some people wrote off Elizabeth's experience as just an emotional one. How shallow our criticism can be when we don't understand. We should all pray that more young people would have an experience like this.

Here are other powerful testimonies to further celebrate what God has done and to challenge you to believe Him for anything.

Eddie Bolton was raised in Milan, Tennessee, around bootleg whiskey and racism, a deadly mixture. The judge referred to him as the meanest man in all of Gibson County. At a young age, Eddie saw his father cheat on his mother, drink heavily and get deeply involved with the local chapter of the Ku Klux Klan. Roots of racism ran deep, and before long Eddie found himself lashing out at anyone who was different from him. He also began drinking—a lot.

While in the U.S. Army, Eddie was introduced to drugs, which added to his aggressive behavior. Later, as a civilian, his brushes with the law included an arrest for counterfeiting and numerous assault and battery charges. Many of his arrests stemmed from drunken brawls. He was shot at and had knives pulled on him—once he even started a fight that left his cousin with a slashed throat.

Eddie followed his father's footsteps and joined the KKK. He wanted his wife, Linda, and their small daughter to attend the meetings, but they refused. His abusive ways eventually led to the breakup of his marriage.

But God had a plan. Linda was saved while watching a Christian TV program, and in 1996 she made the first of many trips to the Pensacola revival. She developed a deep burden to see her husband saved. (They had remarried but were once again headed toward divorce.)

Some men from her church decided to take a busload of guys to Pensacola. Linda pleaded with Eddie to go, but he refused. Yet after continuous pressure, he gave in and agreed to join them.

At the revival, God began dealing with Eddie and his hardened heart started softening. The greatest miracle took place on the 10-hour bus trip back home. A cooler was placed in the aisle of the bus, and the men called it the "mercy seat." Eddie sat there for the entire trip, weeping uncontrollably.

He later told me, "I remember feeling all the hurt I had caused other people. I felt everything for the first time in my life. The years of hatred, my wild lifestyle, the abuse of my wife and kids—it all flashed before my eyes. I felt the pain I had caused Jesus and started crying and just couldn't stop. For 10 hours, all the way home, I cried. God showed me how much He loved me. Even when I was doing all those terrible things, He loved me. I just couldn't get over that. It was the first time I ever realized someone really loved me."

Eddie repented aloud for the suffering he had caused his family and his Savior. What some might call an extremely emotional outburst was actually the cry of a bitter, hate-filled man seeking forgiveness.

Today Eddie and his family are actively involved in church and love God with all their hearts. Eddie sought forgiveness from those he had hurt the most. His testimony was broadcast on national television when he asked the African-American community to forgive him. He had realized the power of the Cross and how Jesus made us all one.

Look what the Lord has done!

EXTREME PERSONAL LESSON:

At the foot of the Cross, we are all equal. The blood of Jesus Christ not only washes us clean from our actions but can also totally alter our attitudes.

Do you have any unsaved family members? Would you like to see revival sweep through your family? Here's a story that should encourage everyone to believe God for revival.

Londa Hankins, a young woman in her mid-20s, attended our Awake America crusade in 1998 at the Reunion Arena in Dallas, Texas. She was living a lukewarm Christian life. Earlier that day she had been standing in a supermarket, reading the back of a jar of chicken noodle soup, when the Lord spoke to her about witnessing to a shopper standing nearby. Londa refused and the lady walked away.

Conviction hit Londa like a load of bricks, and she dropped the jar of soup, scattering glass all over the floor. The mess she left on the store floor didn't hold a candle to the mess in her heart.

That night at the crusade, a chill went through Londa's soul when she heard me say, "Perhaps you were in the grocery store today, holding a jar of soup, when the Lord instructed you to witness to another shopper. You refused. Jesus knows you're here, and He wants you to come—now!"

It was a word of knowledge earmarked by God, and it sent Londa running to the altar where she repented and pleaded to Jesus for another chance. Her sinful, lukewarm lifestyle was replaced with the fire of holiness.

She quickly developed a deep burden for her extended family with an aggressive plan of action. She invited them to the Brownsville Revival, to Awake America meetings and to church crusades. She sent tapes of messages and wrote personal letters—anything that would put them under a shower of repentance preaching. Some responded immediately, others took more time. But her persistence paid off. In just a few short years, more than 25 family members were saved. Their family reunions are now filled with praising God.

Look what the Lord has done! It took a word of knowledge from the pulpit to capture Londa's heart. That may sound unusual to you, but it's exactly what she needed.

Rather than focusing on how strange something seems, we should pray, "Whatever it takes, Jesus, just get a hold of our unsaved family members. Get their attention, Jesus, and bring them home."

EXTREME PERSONAL LESSON:

Don't ever give up on family. Use every means possible to saturate them with God's Word. Their refusal to listen should serve as fuel for the fire. Keep going after them until revival flames are blazing through your family tree.

America's social landscape is salted with the stories of kids gone wild, such as Nadia DeRouen and Joshua Seawall. One lived in Louisiana, the other in North Carolina. They didn't know each other, but they both lived rebellious lives filled with alcohol and drugs.

Nadia had no valid reasons to rebel, but she did anyway. She quit school at the age of 16 and ran away from her Cajun home for days and weeks at a time. She began to lie and steal. Away from home she found plenty of companions; they lived in abandoned houses, slept on benches, in recycling bins, on sidewalks and under bridges.

Nadia's lifestyle even caught the attention of the national media. She appeared, along with her mother, on the Maury Povich TV show. The theme for the program that day was rebellious teenagers who had been kicked out of their homes. Her mother thought that appearing together on the talk show would somehow bridge the gap between them. It didn't—Nadia grew even more rebellious.

She never smiled. She wanted people to fear her rather than love her. During this time she got into the skinhead scene, was a self-proclaimed neo-Nazi and dabbled in witchcraft.

Eventually Nadia got busted and ended up in jail. The night before her court date, she had a close encounter with God and turned her life over to Him. The next day the judge showed leniency, placing her on probation but with serious stipulations. She had to stay clean and attend a series of counseling sessions.

Her sessions were held at a local church that eventually bused her to the Brownsville Revival. She came on Halloween 1996 and was baptized there the next day. She now testifies about how she received true freedom and liberty in Christ at the revival. She saw God for who He really is. He showed her His love, freedom and grace.

Part of her story appeared in the secular music magazine *Spin*. That's where Joshua comes in. In the fall of 1997, Joshua, who was living in full-blown rebellion, went into a music store to buy a CD. He saw the *Spin* magazine with the teaser on the front: "103,000 Saved . . . A Second Coming in Pensacola." He forgot about the CD, bought the magazine, went home, read the article and was profoundly affected.

It was all part of an avalanche of God's love falling upon Joshua. Members of his family were getting saved and faithfully witnessing to him. A cousin started a church in his home and invited Joshua to attend their Bible study. He did and was saved.

Joshua later entered the Brownsville Revival School of Ministry. He started to believe God for the rest of his family. The Lord heard his prayers.

His dad, mom and two sisters were soon saved. His aunt, uncle and cousins came back to Jesus and are now in church. Revival is sweeping through his family.

Thanks, Nadia, for coming to the revival and responding to the Gospel. Thanks, Joshua, for picking up the magazine and reading about the Lord's work. Thanks for yielding to Jesus. Look what the Lord has done! A chain of grace began because of their obedience.

Each of these testimonies is unique. Each reveals the love of Jesus shining forth through different individuals. God can package and deliver His message however He sees fit. Let God be God. Be challenged and dare to be one of those who follow Jesus completely.

**WANTED:
EXTREME
CHRISTIANS**

Leaving a Legacy

CHAPTER TWELVE

EXTREME LESSON:

The way we live our lives here on earth will determine how we are remembered.

"The memory of the righteous is blessed, but the name of the wicked will rot."

PROVERBS 10:7

I'm writing this at sunrise in an airport in Lisbon, Portugal, where we have just completed several days of powerful outdoor crusades. Each night hundreds of people ran to the altars for forgiveness. Our messages were clear and direct: "We're all sinners. Sin separates us from God, but Jesus came to take away our sins. Come to Jesus! He loves you and has a plan for your life."

And they came running. Local pastors said they had never seen anything like it. But we have. All over the world the altars are full, people are weeping, and heaven is rejoicing.

A man told me the other day how much he loved the altar calls at our services. It overwhelmed him with joy to see hundreds rushing forward to receive forgiveness from Jesus. To me, such urgency is real. I preach every message as if it is my last.

This is the hallmark of our ministry. People who knew Jeri and me 20 years ago tell us that our message has not changed. We were passionate about souls back then, and we're still passionate about souls now.

Not only has the Church labeled this ministry as one with evangelistic fervor, but the secular media also seems to agree. Peter Carlson of the *The Washington Post* wrote, "Hill's voice was as a trumpet and his words were as fire."[1]

Lynn Sherr with ABC-TV's *20/20* said, "Hill's urgent call to the altar . . . sends sinners running, a countdown to salvation. Clearly, this is not church as usual."[2]

Remember the article from *Spin* that led to Joshua Seawall's salvation? This is part of what reporter Mark Schone recorded: "From bell to bell, Stephen Hill has his listeners by the scruff of the neck. . . . You have never in your life experienced religion so fulfilling, total and joyful."[3]

In my introduction to this book, I spoke of David Wilkerson, the man who had boldly interrupted a New York City gang trial back in 1958 and then was swiftly escorted from the courtroom to a group of reporters hungry for a good story.

I keep a copy of that article in my study. The headline reads "Preacher Interrupts Gang Murder Trial: Judge Orders Him Taken Out." The article says that Wilkerson was trying to help the boys in the gang by sharing with them about God. It also talked about a large group of young people back in Pennsylvania who were fasting and praying for an open door of ministry. Let me tell you what resulted.

Through this radical, extreme behavior, Wilkerson had unwittingly placed himself in the public spotlight, and the timing couldn't have been better. When the gangs saw the paper, they saw a man who was on their side, and it opened the doors for ministry.

From his fanatical love for youth came the international program Teen Challenge. Little did the media know they were recording the beginning of David Wilkerson's legacy.

Speaking of New York, I'm sure you're familiar with *The New York Times*. Why would such a world-renowned paper make the Brownsville Revival front-page news? Pulitzer-prize-winning writer Rick Bragg wrote: "Stephen Hill reaches for the bleakest sinner with one hand, even as he gropes for the comfortable, social-club Christian with the other. Both, he warns, will bust hell wide open."[4]

Lisa Singh, a reporter for the *Dallas Observer,* followed our team to Houston for a crusade. She wrote: "There's nothing like a Steve Hill altar call. Nothing like hearing him shout with utter urgency for the sinner to 'Hurry!' before he's condemned to that dark place of weeping and gnashing of teeth—hell. Hill lives to save souls."[5]

Friend, I share these quotes for a reason. The secular media is helping document the living legacy of this preacher. Jeri and I have chosen to live our lives in obedience to Christ; to some this is extreme; to us it's normal Christianity. These reporters record-ed the Gospel message for everyone to read, see and hear as it is lived out through faithful people like David Wilkerson.

They record my words. They write about my life. What would they write about you?

EXTREME PERSONAL LESSON:

We are all under observation. We are all being watched. The life you're living—like it or not— is going to be remembered. What kind of legacy will you leave?

When I speak of leaving a legacy, I am referring to the character of the person and the example they leave for others to follow.

For instance, few people would dispute the fact that Mother Teresa left a tremendous legacy when she passed away. She had no financial wealth whatsoever (all of her personal possessions would have fit into one very small suitcase), but her legacy is perhaps greater than those who've left behind vast riches. Her legacy is simple: Give your life to those in need.

Every time Mother Teresa's name comes up, no matter where, people immediately recognize the name of the humble yet strong little woman who cared for the poor and destitute. Her deeds will be taught 100 years from now. She reached out to the impoverished, to those who were hurting. As Scripture states, her memory is blessed: "The memory of the righteous is blessed, but the name of the wicked will rot" (Prov. 10:7).

I imagine most people would prefer to leave the kind of legacy described in the first part of that verse, "The memory of the righteous is blessed." Many, unfortunately, leave the kind mentioned in the latter part, "but the name of the wicked will rot." Remember, a legacy is something you leave behind.

No one in history, including Mother Teresa, left a legacy like Jesus. Nobody. Show me anyone who influenced mankind like Jesus did. But who can equal the Son of God, King of kings and Lord of lords? Show me someone whose life has been the subject of books, songs, illustrations and paintings as much as Jesus' life has.

Pull out a coin and look at the imprinted date. Did you know that our calendar is based on the date of Jesus' birth? Not only is the year of His birth noted, but He was so important that we also use the abbreviation "B.C." (i.e., before Christ) to indicate that period of time before His birth. The period after His birth is referred to as "A.D." and is the abbreviation for the Latin term *Anno Domini* meaning "in the year of our Lord." What a legacy!

Who is this Man who has untold songs composed about Him? You don't hear any songs about Napoleon, Caesar or Abraham Lincoln, but new songs are written all the time about Jesus. He shook this world in His 33 years and made an everlasting impression. During His earthly ministry everybody knew of Him, and when He left, everybody knew He was gone. Now everyone waits for His return.

He left a legacy by the way He lived, by His holiness. "[Jesus] was in all points tempted like as we are, yet without sin" (Heb. 4:15, *KJV*). He was selfless. Not only did He feel others' pain, but He also did something about it.

He left a legacy by the way He died. "Greater love has no one than this, that one lay down his life for his friends" (John 15:13). What a Lord! What love! What a legacy He left for us as an example to follow.

How do people know you? What kind of person are you? How are people talking about you? If you die tonight, how would people remember you? How do people see you react? Are you a faithful friend who sticks around even when the chips are down? What kind of legacy are you leaving?

It's easy to live for Jesus when everything is smooth sailing, but when the storm clouds come, are you blown whichever way the wind is blowing?

Will you be remembered as an on-fire, white-hot, blood-washed believer in Jesus who was unashamed to witness of His love? Are you what some would call an extreme Christian? Or will you be known as a lukewarm, Sunday-morning hypocrite? The choice is yours.

You can be a godly parent who raises children in the love and admonition of the Lord or you can be known as one who is lenient, undisciplined and blames society or the school system for the way the child is turning out. It's your choice.

Teenager, you can be known as promiscuous or as addicted, or you can have the reputation of being a disciplined person who says no when someone peddles sex or drugs.

Yes, you have a choice—live for the world or live for Jesus. Be ashamed of Christ or boldly declare your faith. Hang with godly friends or hang with those you know are bad news. It's a choice, friend, and it will determine your legacy.

There are people who stand out in history for positive reasons, because of what they chose to do with their lives. For example, did you know that Abraham Lincoln did not succeed when he first ran for public office? He failed over and over again, losing election after election, yet he didn't give up. And he went on to become one of our greatest presidents; indeed, he left an honorable legacy.

Booker T. Washington founded the Tuskegee Institute in Alabama in the late 1800s. The school included over 100 buildings, a faculty of 200 and a student body of 1,500. He amassed an endowment of $2 million dollars—an enormous amount of money back then. His book, *Up From Slavery*, changed the perspective of thousands of Americans when it came to prejudice. He left a great legacy.

Evan Roberts, the great Welsh revivalist, is known in the history books as a man who went after God.

Helen Keller, though blind and deaf, became a noted author and lecturer and encouraged countless thousands to persevere in the face of seemingly insurmountable circumstances.

John Wesley, English evangelist and founder of Methodism, endured rotten eggs, rotten fruit, stones and a flurry of bad press for preaching the Gospel. He could have amassed a fortune though his ministry, but he chose to leave a different kind of legacy. He once said, "Whenever I get a little bit of money, I get rid of it as quickly as I can so it won't find a place in my heart."[6]

Johann Sebastian Bach, the great German composer, wrote boldly of the Christian faith in his classic hymns, "Jesus, Joy Of Man's Desiring," "How Joyful Is My Heart," "His Sheep May Safely Graze," "God Alone Should Have My Heart," "Withstand Firmly Against All Sin" and "What God Has Done Is Mightily Done." Though he lived a long time ago, his music and his legacy live on, inspiring the worship and adoration of Jesus Christ.

The story is told of another great composer, George Frideric Handel, who wrote his masterpiece "Messiah" with his Bible open to Isaiah 53:5 (*KJV*), "He was wounded for our transgressions, He was bruised for our iniquities." Handel's eyes welled with tears that dripped on the score he was composing. What passion for Christ! What a legacy to leave for us!

You may be thinking, *Big deal. What do all these dead folks have to do with me?* My friend, look at what's happened. Decades, even centuries later, we still talk about them and remember their lives, their work—it's almost like they're still alive. You, too, can be remembered—on a grand scale or just among your family and friends—as someone who did something for the kingdom of God, somebody whose life meant something.

Or you can leave a negative legacy. Everyone knows whom I'm talking about when I mention Adolf Hitler. His name will

rot just as Scripture said. And Jesus made reference to someone else who left a negative legacy when He said in Luke
17:32, "Remember Lot's wife." She left a different kind of
legacy. When you think of Joseph Stalin, Lee Harvey Oswald,
Jeffrey Dahmer or Timothy McVeigh, you think of negative
legacies.

Yes, you have a choice of how you live your life.

The world was shocked at the events of September 11,
2001. Thousands of innocent lives were lost. In an instant the
pen was laid down. The last page was written. Many were
Christians. Many were not. They all left some type of legacy.

Death is certain for all of us, unless the Lord returns. No one
has a choice about dying. Robert Murray McCheyne said, "It is a
solemn thing to die, because if we die wrong, we cannot come
back to die again."[7]

Sinners laughingly say, "Eat, drink and be merry, for tomorrow we die." However, I have been at the deathbeds of sinners
who, in their last hours, desperately called for the preacher, not
their partying buddies. Your death may be slow or quick, but
regardless, your legacy will have been written by the time you
depart this world.

EXTREME PERSONAL LESSON:

**The way you treat Jesus down here will determine
how He treats you up there. The way you live
your life down here determines where
you'll spend eternity.**

Your legacy, what people will remember about you, is being
written right now.

I have had the privilege of holding crusade meetings in Europe with one of the greatest evangelists of our time, Reinhard Bonnke. He has held some of the largest crusades in history. Recently while we were dining together in Munich, I asked him to tell me about the most dangerous moments of his life. He described the massive crusades he holds in Africa and how, at times, his very life has been threatened. His dramatic stories are always followed by this statement, "But Africa shall be saved!"

The zeal and fire of this man of God will forever leave an impression on my heart. Nothing will stop him from proclaiming the good news of Jesus. His legacy is written.

Dear reader, should you die tonight, your legacy is determined. The story has been written and, like it or not, it will be read.

Here's how Paul felt about his legacy, "I have fought the good fight, I have finished the course, I have kept the faith" (2 Tim. 4:7). It sounds like he knew he was dying but realized he was leaving a God-honoring legacy. He had been shipwrecked, beaten, jailed and persecuted. He had possessed much and he had possessed nothing, and through it all he stood strong.

He then says, "In the future there is laid up for me the crown of righteousness, which the Lord, the righteous Judge, will award to me on that day; and not only to me, but also to all who have loved His appearing" (2 Tim. 4:8). You can have a similar legacy to that of the apostle Paul's—the same crown of righteousness.

I wept with the rest of the Christian world in 1982 when the news came that a small plane had crashed on the Last Days Ministries property in Lindale, Texas. Keith Green and two of his children, Josiah and Bethany, were among those killed.

Keith was one of my heroes. I observed his life and felt his zeal while at Twin Oaks Academy in Lindale—he was one of those people who irritated the Body of Christ. He would tell a congregation, "Everyone here is called to the mission field. You've got to be called *not* to go." Keith bothered ho-hum Christians. He was not one to be passive about anything, and from other Christians He expected no less than total commitment to Jesus.

In one of his Last Days Ministries newsletters he wrote this challenge: "To be a servant of Jesus Christ, an ambassador, a missionary, is the highest calling a man or woman can attain to! What are you waiting for?"[8]

He was buried with Josiah and Bethany in the same casket, one in each arm. "Gone to be with Jesus" is the simple epitaph inscribed on their gravestone. Even though Keith has gone to be with Jesus, when I hear his songs today I realize his music is still preaching the Gospel message—all over the world. What a legacy!

Even more recently, like thousands of others I was saddened when I heard about an accident on a stretch of interstate in rural Illinois. A Jeep carrying two men swerved off the road one night and flipped over. The driver was flung out of the window, and the impact killed him instantly.

Before his sudden death, Rich Mullins had become one of the true poets in the Christian music industry and one of the greatest Christian songwriters of our time. His well-known song "Our God Is an Awesome God" appears in many different denominational hymnals and is sung around the world. Rich's legacy will be with us a long time.

Remember, a righteous man's legacy will be blessed. Every one of these people I've introduced you to—and millions of others too—left behind lasting, godly memories in the hearts of those who knew them. Many have touched the world with their legacies. How about you?

If the story of your life has been dominated by sin, remember that Jesus is willing to erase your past legacy. "If we confess our sins, He is faithful and righteous to forgive us our sins and to cleanse us from all unrighteousness" (1 John 1:9).

God changed my legacy. If I had died during my drug and crime days, I would have left a horrible, wasted legacy—one that would rot and be forgotten in time. God changed all that. When you repent and start walking with Jesus, God promises to restore the years that the locusts have eaten (see Joel 2:25). He will blot out your past legacy.

I was once known for criminal activity; I'm now known for Christian activity. Once a desperate beggar, I am now a dedicated believer. I went from being a young man wasted on booze to a new creature washed in His Blood. Once perishing with the crowd, now I am preaching to the crowd.

Friend, leave a powerful, righteous, devil-defeating legacy. May words like "radical," "intense" and "beyond-the-norm" characterize your life. Be one of those who dare to obey Christ completely. Heaven is hanging posters all over the world that read "Wanted: Extreme Christians." Yes, these are the days for extreme Christianity!

Notes

1. Peter Carlson, "What in God's Name . . .," *The Washington Post*, April 27, 1997, section F, p. 4.
2. Lynn Sherr, *20/20*, October 9, 1997.
3. Mark Schone, *Spin* (September 1997), p. 112.
4. Rick Bragg, "In Florida, a Revival That Came but Didn't Go," *The New York Times*, May 27, 1997, section A, p. 1.
5. Lisa Singh, "The Apostle," *Dallas Observer*, vol. 912 (August 24 30, 2000), p. 34.
6. John Wesley, *Brainy Quote*. http://www.brainyquote.com/quotes/quotes/ j/q106808.html (accessed January 8, 2002).
7. Robert Murray McCheyne, "The Spirit Committed to God," *A Basket of Fragments* (Iverness, Scotland: Christian Focus Publications, n.d.), p. 135.
8. Keith Green, source unknown.

What does it take for a person to make extreme, lasting change in their lives?

How can someone drained by years of addictions, driven by loneliness, and haunted by the past, find extreme peace? Only through a face-to-face encounter with an extreme God. For both Steve and Jeri Hill, that opportunity came over 20 years ago. After years of drug abuse and a long list of other life-controlling issues, the chains of this world were broken off in one act of extreme forgiveness—the forgiveness only found in the love of Jesus Christ. Lasting change came into their lives and they continue to travel the world telling as many as they can reach of the powerful, simple truth that set them free: *Jesus loves you, and has a plan for your life!*

Steve & Jeri Hill
Today

Here are other books from Steve Hill

To order any of these books, for more information about
Together in the Harvest Ministries, Inc. or a
complete resource catalog of books, videos,
and tapes by Steve Hill, write to:

Together in the Harvest Ministries, Inc.

P.O. Box 619777 · Dallas, TX 75261-6177
or visit online at

www.stevehill.org

STONE COLD HEART B001

Stone Cold Heart, Stephen Hill's dramatic story of deliverance from drug addiction and alcoholism, has been published in book form in six languages and distributed to more than 300,000 people around the world. Together in the Harvest has received hundreds of letters from those who have been given a copy by a loving friend or `family member, testifying that their lives were touched and changed by God's deliverance of someone like Steve.

Ardent Press, Inc., Pocket sized, 56 pages $2.00

TIME TO WEEP B002

Are we so hardened by the world around us that our hearts cannot be touched by the things that touch God's heart? Or worse, are we so buried in the 'comforts of Christianity' that we don't really have any idea of what's going on around us? Inside every man and woman there is a fountain waiting to erupt – a fountain so powerful that it produces its own language, the language of tears. It is unleashed when we finally see the reality of who we are in relation to God.

Creation House, 179 pages $12.00

These and other valuable resources from Steve Hill &
Together in the Harvest Ministries are available at www.stevehill.org

WHITE CANE RELIGION

B003

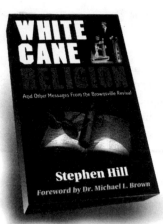

Early in the Brownsville Revival, the Lord emphatically warned Steve to, "Preach what I have placed upon your heart. Do not hesitate or put it off." This compilation of 12 powerful, hard-hitting sermons is a glimpse at some of that preaching. From titles like "Stubborn as a Mule" to "The Romance of Satan," this collection challenges the reader to be on guard and live holy before God.

Revival Press, an imprint of Destiny Image, 165 pages **$12.00**

THE GOD MOCKERS

B004

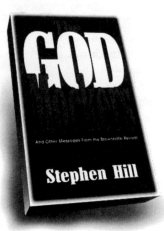

These ten messages incorporate a second collection of the most requested and hard-hitting messages preached during the revival. Included are, the title sermon, "The Sin Mockers," "God Snubs Snots," and "Lucifer's List." Their truth is penetrating. Their simplicity may surprise you. The results are eternal.

Revival Press, an imprint of Destiny Image, 172 pages **$10.00**

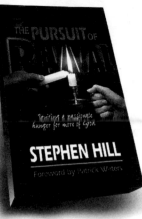

PURSUIT OF REVIVAL B005

Now is the time to pray for a move of God in this land. Don't be lulled to sleep by the "normal Christian life." This powerful book makes it very clear that there is no such thing. Let the Holy Spirit kindle a burning desire in your heart to see your family, your city, your country touched like the thousands who have been radically changed by the power of God through their pursuit of revival.

Creation House, 163 pages **$10.00**

DAILY AWAKENINGS B006

DAILY AWAKENINGS is a 365-day morning devotional which offers a daily challenge and call to holiness—combining the thoughts and teachings of some of the greatest Christian `leaders of the past 400 years—with the fresh fires of revival currently sweeping the land. Many of Hill's powerful sermons are woven throughout this joyous collection of inspirational daily readings, which will encourage, confront and inspire to go deeper in your walk with Jesus.

Regal Publishers, hard cover, 348 pages **$15.00**

These and other valuable resources from Steve Hill &
Together in the Harvest Ministries are available at www.stevehill.org

KNOCKIN' AT HEAVEN'S DOOR

B011

In a day where we find ourselves feeling lost in the depths of a dark and lonely world, Steve Hill throws out a lifeline – the promise of eternal life through Jesus Christ. Many believe in a 'heaven,' but do we know what it really takes to get there? We do not need to change God's truth, but instead, we need to let God's truth change us. With his classic simplicity and down-to-earth style, Hill brings that truth right to the door of your heart with Knockin at Heaven's Door.

Regal Publishers, hard cover, 178 pages

$15.00

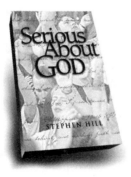

SERIOUS ABOUT GOD

B013

We are living in a day of tremendous spiritual hunger. People don't want to just hear about God, they want to know Him. People are tired of playing church, falling away from God and pursuing their own destruction. This small resource teaches vital elements of a serious beginning in the Lord, overcoming the enemy, and how to live victoriously in Christ! It also serves as good follow-up material for those you may be discipling, or for study in a small-group setting.

Ardent Press, Inc., pocket size, 64 pages

$2.00

These and other valuable resources from Steve Hill &
Together in the Harvest Ministries are available at www.stevehill.org